The
Gourmet Garden

3

The Gourmet Garden

HOW TO GROW VEGETABLES, FRUITS
AND HERBS FOR TODAY'S CUISINE

Theodore James, Jr.

E. P. DUTTON, INC.   NEW YORK

Published in the United States by E. P. Dutton, Inc.,
2 Park Avenue, New York, N.Y. 10016

Library of Congress Cataloging in Publication Data

James, Theodore.
    The gourmet garden.

        1. Vegetable gardening. 2. Fruit-culture.
3. Cookery (Vegetables) 4. Cookery (Fruit)
I. Title.
SB321.J35   1983   635   82-4584
                                  AACR2

ISBN: 0-525-93264-x (cl)
      0-525-48044-7 (pa)

Published simultaneously in Canada by Clarke, Irwin & Company Limited,
Toronto and Vancouver

10 9 8 7 6 5 4 3 2 1
First Edition

For Edith and Francis R. "Ady" Schreiber,
my dear friends who have so generously shared
their vast knowledge of the cultivation and
preparation of fine vegetables with me.

Contents

Acknowledgments   xi
Introduction   xiii

VEGETABLES

Arugula   3
Asparagus   6
Asparagus Beans   11
Beets, Belgian   14
Bok Choy   17
Carrots, Belgian   20
Cayenne Peppers   23
Celeriac   26
Chinese Cabbage   28
Corn   30
Cornichons   33
Cress   36
Eggplant   38
Escarole   41
Finocchio   43
Garlic, Elephant   45
Ginger Root   48
Haricots Verts   51

Horseradish   54
Kipfel Kartoffel   56
Leeks   59
Lettuce   63
Lily Buds   66
Mâche   68
Melon Charantais   70
Onions   73
    Bottle Onions   74
    Globe Onions   75
    Egyptian Onions   76
Paprika Peppers   78
Petits Pois   81
Radish, Oriental Daikon   84
    French Breakfast   86
Rhubarb   88
Romano Beans   91
Shallots   93
Snow Peas   96
Spaghetti Squash   99
Sprouts   102
Sugar Snap Peas   104
Tabasco Peppers   107
Tokyo Turnips   110
Tomato, Cherry   112
    Roma   115
Sorrel   118

HERBS AND SPICES

Anise Seed   123
Basil   125
Caraway Seed   128
Catnip   130
Chervil   132
Chives   135
Dill   138
The Mints   140
Oregano   143
Parsley   145

Rosemary	147
Sage	149
Sesame Seed	151
Tarragon	153
The Thymes	155

BERRIES

Blackberries	161
Blueberries	164
Currants, Black	167
Red	168
Fraises des Bois	171
Gooseberries	174
Raspberries, Red	177
Black and Yellow	182

FRUIT TREES

Apples	189
Apricots	194
Cherries	197
Nectarines and Peaches	200
Pears	204
Plums	208
Figs	212

NUT TREES

Black Walnuts	221
Butternuts	223
Chinese Chestnuts	224
Hardy Hazelnut	225
Shagbark Hickory	226
Carpathian Persian Walnut	227
Hardy Pecan	228
Almond	229

Index	231

Acknowledgments

I would like to express my gratitude to the Belgian National Tourist Office, American Airlines, Pan Am, Trans-World Airlines, Air-Inter, the Chateau du Domaine de St. Martin, Vence, the PLM Terminus Lyon, PLM Le Pigonnet, Aix-en-Provence, PLM Ile Rousse, Bandol, the Paris Sheraton and the Hyatt Nice, and the Hotel Meridien Copacabana in Rio de Janeiro.

Thanks are also due my mother, Mrs. Theodore James, Sr., for assisting with the typing of the manuscript, and my father Theodore James, Sr., for his advice about presentation of the material. Also thanks are due the distinguished photographer Harry Haralambou for his support and encouragement.

Introduction

It has often been said that the difference between America's rich and the rest of the population is that the rich eat tiny, baby vegetables: peas the size of beebees, string beans that resemble darning needles, and carrots the size of a pinky. Undoubtedly, these tendencies to culinary esoterica were acquired in travels on the Continent, for there, almost everybody, rich and poor alike, eats tiny fresh vegetables.

In the United States, vegetables, fruits, and berries are grown to maturity and beyond. They are hybridized to produce heavy yield, and thus more profit, and to be tough enough to endure long-distance travel. Consequently, baby vegetables, vine-ripened fruits and berries, fresh herbs, and the entire category of what is somewhat facetiously called "gourmet vegetables" are rarely, if ever, available in the markets. And so, Americans who have consumed the delectable petits pois or mirabelle plums of France, baby carrots and blanched asparagus in Belgium, fingerling potatoes in Austria, or Oriental vegetables in Chinese or Japanese restaurants think they must do without at home.

On the contrary. These treats are as easily grown in the home orchard as the seeds and plants of "American" varieties which are sold in nurseries and the mature fruits, berries, herbs, and vegetables that are sold in the markets. It is simply a matter of knowing the sources for seeds or plants and perhaps a few, specific requirements.

To begin with, I will not attempt to give you instructions in basic gardening techniques. I assume that if you are interested in moving on to more unusual vegetables you have already had a reasonable amount of gardening experience. In other words, you know what Rototilling is, you know how to cultivate with a hoe, you are aware that compost is like gold. And you know that if it doesn't rain for a week that it's time to drag out the hose and sprinkle.

And, rather than discussing planting, cultivation, watering, pruning, harvesting, pest and disease control, mulching, fertilizing, and other aspects of gardening in separate chapters of this book, all instructions pertaining to each vegetable, herb, fruit, berry, or nut are included in each individual entry. I think you'll find this a far more convenient way to learn about growing varieties you opt to plant rather than having to thumb through cross-references and appendixes.

You will notice as you read through this book that many "Gardener's Tips" are included at the end of each entry. Do not ignore them. They include advice garnered from many experienced sources through the years, as well as my own comments. They will help you to succeed with your garden.

And then, I have also included "Cooking Tips," suggestions or recipes concerned with the preparation of your crops for eating and preserving. These tips are by no means intended to be the last word on preparing all of these treats. Consult your favorite cookbooks for further suggestions.

Before moving on, mention should be made of the growing interest in organic gardening. You might wish to consider growing your produce in this manner. I expect it can be said that crops grown organically taste better and are more healthful not only for you but for the environment as well. For this reason, right at the start, I include a formula for an organic fertilizer which you may choose to use rather than the chemically produced 5-10-5.

There are dozens of combinations of organic materials which will produce a good balanced fertilizer. One particularly good mixture which should serve you well follows:

In an 8-gallon container prepare your fertilizer mix. The proportion should be roughly 30 percent dried sheep or cow manure (horse manure is not recommended until it has been thoroughly composted for one year), 20 percent good compost or peat moss, 10 percent bloodmeal, 10 percent bonemeal, 15 percent superphosphate or natural rock phosphate, 10 percent ground limestone, and 5 percent vermiculite. Use this instead of 5-10-5 fertilizer, roughly doubling the amount specified for each application.

Again, in keeping with the trend away from chemical pesticides, pests and diseases can be controlled, to a degree, with nontoxic or organic substances. I will stress this aspect of control throughout the book whenever practical. As a rule of thumb, when you plan your garden, interplant among your crops the following: old-fashioned French marigolds, nasturtiums, herbs of all varieties, and garlic—lots of it. They all help to ward off pests and disease.

One final bit of preliminary advice for general gardening of all kinds. Put up a fence! And make that fence high enough (4 feet is minimum) with dense enough mesh to ward off rabbits, stray dogs, and other animals. The investment is quite small compared to the damage that several rabbits or dogs can wreak in a season or two, let alone overnight. Your fence will also serve as a trellis for peas, beans, tomatoes, cucumbers, and melons, conserving space and saving time and trouble in fashioning supports for individual crops. If deer are a problem in your area, make your fence 8 feet tall, and if woodchucks are a local pest, bury your fence 1 foot deep.

A postscript: Remember your friends. That is, the insects, birds, and reptiles that will help you in your pursuit of growing fine produce. If you are a gardener, you undoubtedly feed the birds during the winter. Continue to do so in the summer. Oh, yes, there are some delectables that they enjoy. But the birds will repay you times ten by eating hundreds of thousands of undesirable insects. Do not kill toads or garter snakes; they consume their weight in pests every week. Learn which insects are beneficial to your garden. These include ladybugs, praying mantis, ground beetles, the iridescent blue-green European ground beetle, and the tiger beetle. Also the robber fly, assassin bug, golden-eyed lacewing, ant-lion (also called doodlebug), damsel bug, syrphid fly (also called flower fly), and the wasp. They attack and kill many pests that rob you of food.

So then, if you can't resist the temptation to treat yourself to the best that nature has to offer, read on, for this book will teach you most of what you must know to enjoy the remarkable bounty of a garden of wonderful vegetables, fruits, berries, herbs, and nuts.

Vegetables

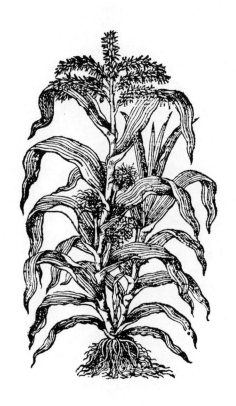

Arugula

ROQUETTE OR ROCKET

HARDINESS: Annual, very hardy.

WHEN TO PLANT: In early spring, as soon as ground is workable, then successively every 10 days throughout the season.

SPACING: Rows about 1 foot apart; plant seeds thinly.

DEPTH: 1/4 inch.

HARVEST TIME: Anywhere from 3 to 5 weeks. Arugula will go to seed after about 6 weeks.

The peppery tang of arugula (or roquette or rocket) is ubiquitous on the tables of elegant northern Italian restaurants, or for that matter on al fresco tables of Italian peasants in the same district. Occasionally this vegetable is available in ethnic markets at reasonable prices, or in posh food emporiums at exorbitant prices. Grow it yourself. It is virtually disease- and pest-free, foolproof to cultivate, and a delight to the palate. Considering that a package of seeds will cost you about sixty-five cents, as compared to a four-dollar salad order at a posh New York City restaurant, and further considering that your package of seeds, with a minimum of care, will probably produce enough salads to turn the Italian navy green, well . . . enough said.

3

HOW TO GROW ARUGULA

Plant in full sun as soon as ground is workable and then every 10 days for a continuous supply of young leaves. Sow tiny seeds rather thinly about 1/4 inch deep. You would do well to mix the seeds with sand before sowing in order to ensure a thinly sowed crop. Cover with soil and keep well watered until seeds germinate. You should be able to pick some of your crop in about 4 weeks to add zest to salads. After that, you can pick young leaves and make a salad using only arugula. This plant goes to seed in about 6 weeks, so plan on successive plantings.

GARDENER'S TIP 1

As the plants bolt, pull them out of the soil. Quality deteriorates as the plant ages. However, if you plant successive crops, you should not have to be without plenty of this delicious salad ingredient all through the season.

GARDENER'S TIP 2

As the season draws to a close, be sure to allow some of your plants to go to seed. Collect the seeds, and store over the winter in airtight containers in a cool, dark place. The back of the refrigerator will do. Once in the refrigerator, be sure not to confuse your arugula seeds with leftovers and throw them out.

PESTS: Mercifully, none.

VARIETIES: Demonchaux's is called Roquette Cultivee.

SOURCE: These days, arugula, generally sold under the name of rocket or roquette, appears quite regularly in the seed racks of your local garden center. By mail order: J. A. Demonchaux Co., Inc., 827 North Kansas, Topeka, Kansas 66608.

COOKING TIP 1

If you have not yet acquired a taste for arugula, try some mixed with romaine, Boston, or leaf lettuce in a salad. You'll find that before long, you'll crave more, ultimately finding a pure arugula salad to your liking. It is also delectable when combined with sliced beefsteak tomatoes in a vinaigrette dressing.

COOKING TIP 2

As arugula ages, the leaves become somewhat tough and are really no longer desirable for salads. However, at that stage of their maturity, they are excellent in soups. Consult any basic Chinese cookbook for an egg drop soup recipe. Then, instead of adding bok choy to the soup, add a reasonable amount of arugula to it.

Asparagus

HARDINESS: Perennial, very hardy.

WHEN TO PLANT: In early spring, as soon as ground is workable.

SPACING: Set plants 18 inches apart in rows 2 feet apart.

DEPTH: Initially from 6 to 8 inches.

HARVEST TIME: 2 years sparingly, then 3 years until July.

In Europe, almost all asparagus is blanched; consequently it is a very pale yellow-green color when in the markets, as compared to our deep green, purple-tipped specimens. I traveled to the heart of the Belgian asparagus country to see firsthand just how the blanching process is accomplished. Instructions are included below. Keep in mind that blanched asparagus has a different taste from our domestic product. Frankly, I prefer our own version, but on occasion, especially during the height of the season, the change to the blanched vegetable is refreshing. And to the point of absurdity, a friend returning from Paris last spring reported that a side dish of six spears of blanched asparagus cost thirty-five dollars at the Plaza-Athenée Hotel. Enough? Here's how it's done.

HOW TO GROW BLANCHED ASPARAGUS

Asparagus, considered by many to be the "king of vegetables," is among the first spring vegetables to grow in your garden. Plan on an area about 20 feet square, or a row from 50 to 75 feet long for a family of five or six persons. Should you care to can or freeze a supply, a larger plot will be necessary. Unfortunately, top-quality asparagus will not grow in the Deep South because the vegetable needs winters cold enough to freeze the ground at least several inches. You may have some luck growing asparagus in Virginia, the Carolinas, or Kentucky, especially if you live in an area with a high elevation.

Any well-drained fertile soil is good ground for asparagus. Plan on locating your patch in full sun. Preparing the bed requires a reasonable amount of work, but keep in mind that once planted, your asparagus bed will produce for twenty-five to thirty years.

Dig a trench 14 to 16 inches deep. Fill the bottom 6 inches of the trench with rotted manure, leaf mold, rotted leaves, and compost. Then add from 5 to 10 pounds of 5-10-5 fertilizer or from 10 to 20 pounds of organic mixture to each 75-foot row. Work in the soil removed until the trench level is 6 inches below the surrounding soil line. Mix the soil, organic matter, and fertilizer with a cultivator.

You will get quicker and more satisfactory results if you purchase one-year-old asparagus plants from a garden center or through the mail order nurseries than if you plant from seed. If you purchase your plants from a nursery, be sure they are not dried out. They should have a root spread of at least 15 inches, the larger the better. Buy only reliable strains. When the soil is ready for planting, place the crowns of the asparagus at least 1 1/2 feet apart in rows 2 feet apart, and the same distance apart if you plant a bed. Cover the crowns with an inch or two of soil. During the season, as the asparagus spears grow, gradually fill in the rest of the trench until it is at surrounding soil level.

Clean cultivation will encourage growth, so keep your asparagus bed weeded from the start. Hand weeding is probably the best way to do this, but if you use a pre-emergent annual weed killer before the spears appear, the job will be easier.

Do not cut your asparagus the first year. The second year cut only to the beginning of June. The third year, cut until the beginning of July. Be sure to cut every single spear during the cutting period. Then, allow the asparagus to grow undisturbed. In the fall remove the dead tops and dispose of them, as they harbor the asparagus beetle.

Every spring, either before or after the cutting season, fortify your 75-foot row of asparagus with from 6 to 8 pounds of 5-10-5 fertilizer or your organic mixture. Also add compost or rotted manure. It is near impossible to overfertilize asparagus, as the plant is a very heavy feeder.

HOW TO BLANCH ASPARAGUS

In Belgium, the asparagus fields resemble burial grounds for cobra snakes. Mounds of earth about a foot in height stretch from one end of the fields to the other. If you want to try blanching asparagus, you must cover your already established rows before the third-year spears emerge. Place one foot of very friable soil on top of each row. Each mound should be about 1 foot wide at the top, and perhaps 1 1/2 feet wide at the bottom. As soon as cracks appear in the top of the mound, you can assume the asparagus is ready for cutting. Gently move some of the earth mound to be sure. Then insert a very long knife into the mound about 9 or 10 inches below the top and cut. Pull the spear out of the soil and re-firm the mound with your hands. I strongly suggest that if you wish to grow blanched asparagus, you start out on a small scale. Mound about 10 feet of your established row to see if you enjoy the blanched variety as well as the green. If you do, you can always mound more of your row the following year. And then, if you don't care for it, you can remove the 10-foot-long mound in the fall.

GARDENER'S TIP 1

Fertilize, fertilize, fertilize. It is the secret to a bumper crop.

GARDENER'S TIP 2

Be sure your cutting tool is razor sharp so that you don't disturb the rest of the plant.

GARDENER'S TIP 3

Again, and most important, once the bed is established, do not cut after the beginning of July.

GARDENER'S TIP 4

Once you have ceased cutting and let your plants grow to their seasonal maturity, be sure to cut off all stalks bearing berries just below the berry line. This assures that the strength of the plant will not go into producing seeds, but rather will develop a stronger root system.

GARDENER'S TIP 5

Remove any seedlings which may have sprung up in or near your asparagus patch. The offspring may not grow true to their parents. Offspring may harbor asparagus rust, which will affect your plants negatively.

PESTS: Asparagus rust and asparagus beetles are the chief enemies of the plant. Rust-resistant varieties are the answer to avoiding the disease. Asparagus beetles can be picked off the plants by hand.

VARIETIES: Purchase only Mary Washington or Waltham Washington, both rust-resistant. Waltham Washington is a recent improvement on Mary Washington, with spears a deep green with a trace of purple. Asperges d'Argenteuil, a French variety, is available as seeds.

SOURCE: Most garden centers stock roots in early spring. Most mail order nurseries also ship them at the proper time.

COOKING TIP 1

A considerable number of food experts in the world consider the cuisine of Belgium superior to that of France. The Restaurant Bruneau on the Avenue Broustin in Brussels serves the classic Belgian dish, Asparagus à la Flamande, in this manner. The tender white asparagus is presented with a sauce. To make the sauce, crush four hard-cooked eggs in a small bowl. Add 1 cup melted butter, 2 tablespoons minced parsley, and 1 tablespoon fresh lemon juice or 1/8 teaspoon freshly ground nutmeg. Salt and pepper to taste. Serve the sauce in a sauceboat along with about 1 pound of the steamed blanched asparagus. You can also serve this sauce with our American green asparagus.

COOKING TIP 2

At family gatherings in Belgium, the hard-cooked egg is served on a plate. Each person takes one and mashes it himself. The other ingredients are served in a sauceboat and passed around for each diner to sprinkle on his mashed egg and asparagus.

Asparagus Beans

YARD-LONG BEANS
OR DOW GAUK

HARDINESS: Annual, tender.

WHEN TO PLANT: In late spring, mid-May to early June, when all danger of frost is over. Like other bean seeds, these will rot in cool, damp weather.

SPACING: Like domestic pole beans, plant around a 6-foot pole, about 2 inches apart.

DEPTH: One to 2 inches.

HARVEST TIME: Around 45 to 55 days after planting and then throughout the summer and fall until a killing frost.

These Chinese vegetables are different in taste from our domestic pole beans. They have a zippy, nutty, pealike taste which some liken to asparagus. Actually, they are not a member of the bean family, but of the cow pea family. And the nice thing about them is that the plants keep bearing all summer long and into the fall, as long as you continue to pick them as they form. They also freeze well for winter use.

HOW TO GROW ASPARAGUS BEANS

Cultivation is the same as for domestic pole beans. Like most vegetables, these require full sun and a reasonably fertile soil. Do not feed heavily, but a side dressing of 5-10-5 fertilizer or organic mixture will do no harm. Just sprinkle a handful around the base of the plants once they have emerged. Hammer your 6-foot pole into the ground before you plant the beans. Then dig a circle about 1 to 2 inches in depth and plant the seeds 2 to 3 inches apart. Cover with soil and tamp down. When the seedlings are 2 to 3 inches high, pull out every other one. Cultivate to keep free of weeds throughout the growing season and water deeply during drought.

GARDENER'S TIP 1
As with all beans, rabbits are perhaps your chief enemy. Be sure to enclose your garden with fence.

GARDENER'S TIP 2
Pick young for the most tender and flavorful vegetables. You will do well to check your plants daily, as these vegetables grow substantially overnight.

GARDENER'S TIP 3
Do not cultivate these beans when morning dew is on them. Bean rust, if present, will be spread.

GARDENER'S TIP 4
Sometimes these seeds take up to a month to germinate. Do not despair if the seedlings have not emerged after 2 weeks. Be patient.

GARDENER'S TIP 5
At the end of the season, and before killing frost, let some of the plants fully mature. Then pick the pods, dry them, and remove the seeds for next year's crop.

GARDENER'S TIP 6
Most experts agree that inoculating bean and pea seeds before planting ensures very good plant growth, which in turn results in higher yields. The process sounds complicated but it isn't at all. Simply purchase some inoculant from your garden center and proceed as follows. Moisten the seeds, pour on the inoculant powder, roll the seed in the powder, coating it generously, and

plant the seed. The inoculant is a bacteria powder that helps the seed do its job of taking nitrogen from the air and storing it in the plant's root nodules.

PESTS: Apparently there are none.

VARIETIES: Asparagus Bean, Dow Gauk, or Yard-Long Bean

SOURCES: Tsang and Ma International, P.O. Box 294, Belmont, California 94002; Kitazawa Seed Co., 356 W. Taylor St., San Jose, California 95110.

COOKING TIP 1

These beans are delicious stir-fried. Cut them in 1 1/2-inch lengths. Stir-fry 1 minute. Add 2 tablespoons water. Cover 2 to 3 minutes. Add 1 chopped chili pepper and 2 teaspoons brown bean sauce for a taste treat.

COOKING TIP 2

Asparagus beans are also deliciously refreshing when pickled. To prepare, marinate 1 pound beans in 2 tablespoons salad or olive oil, 2 tablespoons water, 2 tablespoons cider vinegar, some grated onion, and some fresh dill. Let sit in the refrigerator overnight and serve chilled.

Beets, Belgian

HARDINESS: Annual, hardy.

WHEN TO PLANT: In early spring, as soon as ground is workable.

SPACING: Rows 14 inches apart, six seeds per foot.

DEPTH: 1/2 to 1 inch.

HARVEST TIME: 7 to 8 weeks.

Indeed in America we've developed some delicious beets, including the golden variety, a yellow beet that is surprisingly tasty. But the Belgians grow strains that are at their flavorful peak when less than 1 inch across. As with so many of these epicurean treats, there is no special cultivation needed. If you grow standard Detroit or Harvard beets, you can grow these Belgian varieties.

HOW TO GROW BELGIAN BEETS

Plant early in full sun, as beets do not thrive in hot weather. And plan on putting in another row or so every 2 weeks to ensure a good supply for the table through most of the summer. First, to encourage rapid growth, remove all stones, twigs, and other trash from the soil. Mix in 3 pounds of 5-10-5 fertilizer per 100-foot row or 6 pounds of your organic mixture plus compost, lime if needed, and rotted manure. Beets also respond well to wood ashes, so if you burn wood in your fireplace or stove, save the ashes during the winter and add to the soil in spring. They are approximately 50 percent lime.

Using the handle of your hoe or rake, dig a furrow no more than 1 inch deep and drop the seeds in six per foot. If your soil bakes to an impenetrable surface after a light rain, cover the seeds with a mixture of peat moss and sand instead of soil. Keep the seedlings well watered and remove weeds by cultivating. Mulch with grass clippings, straw, or sawdust. Remember that the last two mulches draw nitrogen from the soil, which must be returned by fertilizing during the growing season.

When the small roots begin to penetrate above the soil, probably in 7 to 8 weeks, check the size of the beets to determine whether or not they are ready for harvesting. Ideally, they should measure about 1 inch in diameter.

PESTS: Two pests attack beets. Leaf spot will cause small round spots with light-colored centers on the leaves. Crop rotation will help to cut down on this problem. Leaf miners may also attack beets. These are yellow creatures about 1/8 inch in length that tunnel within the leaves. Other than interplanting insect-repellent plants such as garlic, herbs, marigold, and nasturtium, maintaining a clean garden, relying on birds, reptiles and friendly insects, there does not seem to be a nonhazardous way to rid yourself of these pests. Two teaspoons of malathion to 1 gallon of water should be sprayed on the leaves as soon as any evidence of the insect is noticed. Do not spray for 7 days before harvest.

VARIETIES: Flat Egyptian (Rouge-Noir Plate d'Egypte) is the earliest, with Red Capaudine a longer variety with a very sweet taste.

SOURCE: J. A. Demonchaux Co., Inc., 827 North Kansas, Topeka, Kansas 66608.

COOKING TIP 1
Should you have to thin the beets to six per foot, the beet greens which you pull can be prepared like spinach. They are delicious cooked this way.

COOKING TIP 2

Aside from the usual beet with orange glaze or beets with dill, you can also prepare these beets with sour cream as they do in Middle Europe. Here's how you do it. Take 2 cups of boiled beets, sliced or whole, and add 2 tablespoons butter, 1 tablespoon lemon juice, 1/2 teaspoon salt, a dash of freshly ground pepper, 3/4 teaspoon caraway seed, and 1/4 cup sour cream. Place all ingredients in a saucepan and heat, but do not boil. Serve immediately.

Bok Choy

PAK CHOI

⌀

HARDINESS: Annual, very hardy.

WHEN TO PLANT: In early spring, as soon as the ground is workable, or late summer.

SPACING: In rows 1 foot apart. Sow ten seeds per foot. Thin to 6 inches apart.

DEPTH: 1/4 inch.

HARVEST TIME: About 45 days, when choy is 10 to 14 inches tall, just before plant flowers.

If you cook in the Chinese manner, you know that bok choy is basic to that cuisine. It is easily grown as a spring crop, if you know where to get the seeds. Bok choy, like lettuce and spinach, will bolt in hot weather, so plant in early spring or for a fall crop.

HOW TO GROW BOK CHOY

Plant as soon as the ground is workable, or in the cool weather of autumn. Bok choy likes full sun, reasonable moisture, and a fertile soil fortified with rotted manure, compost, and some 5-10-5 fertilizer or organic mixture. Plant the seeds in full sun about 1/4 inch deep and sow them about ten to the foot. The seeds will germinate in about 10 to 15 days. When the seedlings are 3 inches high, thin to 6 inches apart. Fertilize lightly every 2 weeks or so with a side dressing of 5-10-5 fertilizer or organic mixture. After about a month you will be able to cut some of the loose green leaves from the plant. Later you can cut the center stalk or heart. One nice thing about bok choy is that through the cutting season the plant will replenish itself. New leaves and a new heart will grow from the cuttings. When the heat of summer arrives, bok choy will bolt to seed.

GARDENER'S TIP 1
Rabbits relish bok choy, so be sure to enclose your patch with a fence.

GARDENER'S TIP 2
Be sure to allow one plant to go to seed. The seed forms in a pod. When it is dry, crack it open, remove the seeds, and store in a cool, dry place for sowing in the fall or the following spring.

PESTS: Other than rabbits, few pests attack bok choy.

VARIETIES: Several, all nonhybrid. They're all good.

SOURCES: Tsang and Ma International, P.O. Box 294, Belmont, California 94002; Kitazawa Seed Co., 356 W. Taylor St., San Jose, California 95110.

COOKING TIP 1
In China and Japan, people dry a substantial amount of their bok choy crop for use during the winter. When the plant is mature, and before it goes to seed, pull it out and remove the roots. Leave the leaves on the plant, but you can remove the tender heart for immediate use. Wash the vegetable, boil it for 5 to 10 minutes, then hang it up on the clothesline to dry for 5 or 6 days. Each night, bring the crop into the house and cover it with plastic. When it is dry, wrap it and store in a cool, dry place.

COOKING TIP 2
Bok choy is delicious in egg drop soup. After you've heated 1 pint chicken broth, add 3 tablespoons cornstarch diluted in 1/4 cup water. Heat and stir until soup is clear. Bring to a boil and add

sliced stems of bok choy. Then add 1 beaten egg and stir. Finally add chopped bok choy leaves to the soup.

COOKING TIP 3

I have also substituted bok choy for celery in a cold bay scallop salad. The taste is infinitely more subtle than celery, permitting the delicate taste of the scallops to dominate the salad.

Carrots, Belgian

AMSTEL CAROTES

HARDINESS: Annual, hardy.

WHEN TO PLANT: In early spring, as soon as ground is workable, and every 2 weeks for successive crops.

SPACING: Rows about 1 foot apart. Sow tiny seed thinly—ultimately you will have to thin the plant to 2 to 3 inches apart.

DEPTH: 1/2 inch.

HARVEST TIME: 8 to 10 weeks.

Indeed our California carrots are splendid, but you've probably seen packages of tiny orange carrots imported from Belgium in the frozen food section of your supermarket. And one dollar for a small package is not unusual. Well, you can grow them at home as easily as domestic varieties. But, after about 6 weeks, be sure to pull several to see if they are ready to eat, as these carrots must be harvested young to be at their best.

HOW TO GROW BELGIAN CARROTS

Perhaps the most important thing to remember when preparing your carrot bed is to remove all rocks and debris from the soil. If you do not, chances are the roots will be deformed when you pull your crop. Since these vegetables are very small, you won't have to prepare the soil too deeply; however, if your soil is heavy, you might consider adding sizable quantities of vermiculite or, even better, perlite to the soil to lighten it, thus creating a more favorable medium in which to grow them. Work in compost, rotted manure, and 5-10-5 fertilizer or organic mixture.

To plant the seeds, pick a spot in full sun. Make a shallow furrow with the end of a hoe or rake and plant the seeds about 1/2 inch deep. Keep the bed well watered and cultivated throughout the growing season. You will probably have to spend some time hand-weeding between the plants. When seedlings are about 2 inches high, thin to every 2 or 3 inches. After 6 weeks, pull several carrots to determine if they are ready for harvest. If they measure about 3 to 4 inches long and perhaps 1/2 inch to 3/4 inch across they are ready for eating, cooking, or freezing.

GARDENER'S TIP 1
To facilitate planting the tiny seeds, mix with sand before sowing.

GARDENER'S TIP 2
Carrot seeds are very slow in germinating, so don't worry if several weeks pass before you see the tiny green shoots emerging from the soil. Many gardeners mix radish seed with their carrots in order to mark the rows and to harvest a double crop from the same garden area. Radish is ready for harvest in about 3 weeks from planting time, so by the time you've pulled your radishes, the carrots will be ready to claim the space.

GARDENER'S TIP 3
During dry spells, water thoroughly, as carrots need a great deal of moisture to develop properly.

GARDENER'S TIP 4
In the case of carrots, the biggest is not the best, unless of course you plan on making hatchet soup. (Hatchet soup was made in pre-Revolutionary Russia by soldiers stranded in Siberia. It consisted of boiling water, one immense carrot, one very large potato, and one monumental turnip with a rusty hatchet thrown in to add some color.) No! Pick them small and enjoy them.

PESTS: Carrots are generally pest-free; however, you may have a problem with any of the following: Carrot caterpillars are seldom so numerous that you can't hand-pick them. To avoid leaf blight, rotate crops and avoid excessive moisture. Wireworm, a yellowish white worm with dark head and tail, 1/2 to 1 1/2 inches long, tunnels into stems and roots; plant winter rye and turn under in the spring. The soil bacteria which attack the rye are thought to attack wireworms.

VARIETIES: Amstel is the variety you are looking for.

SOURCES: J. A. Demonchaux Co., Inc., 827 North Kansas, Topeka, Kansas 66608.

COOKING TIP 1
At Le Pigeonneau, a charming inn in Aix-en-Provence, France, carrots are julienned, combined with julienned potatoes, and deep-fried as you would American hash brown potatoes. A spinach stuffing is placed in the middle just before serving. The colorful orange of the carrots and golden brown of the potatoes is very appealing to the eye, and the combination of tastes quite special.

Cayenne Peppers

HARDINESS: Annual, tender.

WHEN TO PLANT: Start seeds indoors 6 to 8 weeks before all danger of frost is past. Set outside from mid-May to early June.

SPACING: Indoors: Sow 1 inch apart; outdoors: Plant seedlings 2 feet apart.

DEPTH: Indoors: 1/2 inch; outdoors: Plant seedlings about 1/2 to 1 inch deeper than soil line of seedlings.

HARVEST TIME: In July or August, when peppers are red and ripe.

Cayenne pepper is made from these peppers and, like paprika, is hotter and more flavorful when fresh. In order to make your own, all you must do is raise the pepper plant according to instruction and follow the instructions in the "Cooking Tip" section of this entry. It is no more difficult to grow cayenne peppers than the sweet bell peppers you probably grow now. The red cayenne pepper grows to about 5 inches long and 1/2 inch thick and is often curled and twisted. It is very hot.

HOW TO GROW RED CAYENNE PEPPERS

Start seed indoors in flats filled with a mixture of sand, peat moss, and vermiculite. Sow about 6 to 8 weeks before setting plants out in permanent position in the garden in mid-May or early June, when danger of frost is over. Plant them about 1/2 inch deep, 1 inch apart, water the planting medium thoroughly, and place them in a warm place, about 70 to 80 degrees.

About 1 week later, the seeds will have germinated. Place the flat next to a sunny window, southern exposure preferred. If you have Gro-Lux or fluorescent lights, place the plants under them for about 12 to 14 hours a day.

About a week before outdoor planting time, begin to harden off your plants. Place them outside in the sunshine for a few days and bring them in at night. After they have spent several days outdoors, you can leave them out overnight as long as the temperatures are not too cold, that is below 50 degrees or so.

When all danger of frost is over, and when the seedlings are big enough to handle, plant them 24 inches apart in a sunny spot with well-drained fertile soil. All peppers like a light, friable soil without too much nitrogen. If there is an excess of this element, the plants will go to leaf with little vegetable production. Transplant them on a cloudy day if possible, to avoid wilting from strong sun. Water thoroughly when planting and throughout the growing season.

The problem of cutworm, if truly it is a problem, is included here, rather than in the pest section, as a simple precaution at planting time will save your pepper plants from the ravages of this pest. Cutworms eat the tender stems of peppers, tomatoes, and eggplant. In a single night, they can level your entire planting of young peppers. Simply fashion a collar out of cardboard, aluminum foil, or old tin cans and insert it about 1 inch below soil level to about 3 inches above soil level. This will protect your plant.

By July, your pepper plants will produce small fruits which will slowly turn brilliant red. When they are red and ripe, pick them and prepare for drying.

GARDENER'S TIP 1
Pepper plants are attractive; if space is at a premium, work them into your flower garden or border.

PESTS: If blossom-end rot attacks your plants, dark, sunken leathery spots will appear on the blossom end of the fruit. This problem is likely to occur after dry spells during early growth. Regular watering will probably spare you this outrage.

VARIETY: Long Red Cayenne Pepper.

SOURCE: W. Atlee Burpee Co., Warminster, Pennsylvania 18974, or Clinton, Iowa 52732.

COOKING TIP 1
To make dried cayenne peppers, use only the "walls" of the peppers. Seeds, tissue, and stems are not suitable. Place the "walls" on a screen in a warm, shady, dry place and allow them to dry out. Or dry them in a slow oven (150 degrees) until brittle. When they are bone dry, grind them with a food processor or by hand with a mortar and pestle. Store in glass jar or other moisture-proof container in the refrigerator. For spanking fresh cayenne pepper, place the brittle "walls" in the refrigerator and grind the spice as needed.

Celeriac

TURNIP-ROOTED CELERY

HARDINESS: Annual, hardy.

WHEN TO PLANT: In early spring, as soon as ground is workable.

SPACING: In rows 1 1/2 feet apart; plant seeds thinly, about 1/2 inch apart, and then to 6 inches when 3 inches high.

DEPTH: 1/2 inch.

HARVEST TIME: In the fall or, if wintered over, in very early spring.

The classic French creation, celery rémoulade, is made from this white root. It is rarely available in the markets but is easily grown in your garden. Unlike celery, which is somewhat difficult to grow, celeriac will thrive if given a reasonable amount of attention.

HOW TO GROW CELERIAC

Allow plenty of time for growing, as celeriac requires a long season to mature. Plant in full sun, in early spring as soon as ground is workable—that is when you plant onions, peas, and spinach. Fortify the soil with plenty of rotted manure, compost, and 5-10-5 fertilizer or organic mixture. The seed is small and requires some time to germinate, so soak overnight in water to help speed the process. To facilitate sowing, mix the wet seed with dry sand and distribute it evenly in your planting row. Sow seeds about 1/2 inch apart, 1/2 inch deep. Cover with soil, tamp down, and lightly sprinkle the bed with water. When the seedlings are about 3 inches high, thin to 6 inches. During the growing season, cultivate and water abundantly during periods of drought. Harvest in the fall, or provide winter protection by banking with soil and covering with piles of dead leaves. Dig during the winter or early spring for fresh celeriac.

GARDENER'S TIP 1
If you wish, in the fall you can dig your celeriac crop, cut off the tops, and store the roots in a box of moist sand. Place the box in a cool, dry cellar.

PESTS: Few, if any.

VARIETIES: Alabaster, Large Smooth Prague.

SOURCES: W. Atlee Burpee, Co., Warminster, Pennsylvania 18974, or Clinton, Iowa 52732; Nichols Garden Nursery, 1190 North Pacific Highway, Albany, Oregon 97321; George W. Park Seed Co., Greenwood, South Carolina 29647.

COOKING TIP 1
Jean and Pierre Troisgros, in their book on nouvelle cuisine, suggest using celeriac as garnish for duck livers or, in lieu of that, for chicken livers. The celeriac is diced and then trimmed to olive shapes. It is plunged into a pot of salted, boiling water and rapidly boiled, uncovered, for 6 minutes. Then it is removed, drained, doused in cold water, and drained again. After the preparation of your favorite liver dish, simply scatter the celeriac over the dish and serve.

Chinese Cabbage

SIEW CHOY AND YA CHOY

HARDINESS: Annual, very hardy.

WHEN TO PLANT: In early spring, as soon as the ground is workable, or late summer.

SPACING: In rows 1 foot apart. Sow six seeds per foot and thin to 6 inches apart.

DEPTH: 1/2 inch.

HARVEST TIME: About 80 days, before plants bolt.

Chinese cabbage is basic to Oriental cooking. It's easily grown as a spring crop. Like bok choy and most other Oriental leafy vegetables, Chinese cabbage cannot abide hot weather, so plant early in the spring or for a crop in the fall.

HOW TO GROW CHINESE CABBAGE

Plant the seeds in a sunny spot in the spring as soon as the ground is workable, about the same time you plant lettuce, peas, and onions. Fortify the soil with rotted manure, compost, and 5-10-5 fertilizer or organic mixture. Plant seeds about 1/2 inch deep, in rows 1 foot apart. Sow six seeds per foot; when the plants are 3 inches tall, thin to 6 inches apart. Lightly fertilize with 5-10-5 fertilizer or organic mixture about every 3 weeks during the growing season. As the plants grow larger, tie the leaves together to blanch the vegetable. Of the two varieties, siew choy and ya choy, ya choy is the sweeter vegetable.

GARDENER'S TIP 1
Chinese cabbage will bolt in hot weather, so plant early and pick before going to seed. Let one plant go to seed and collect the seeds for next year's planting.

PESTS: Flea beetles and leaf hoppers may attack the leaves of your plants. Nontoxic natural rotenone will control these. Aphids can be attacked with a peppery spray from your hose.

VARIETIES: Siew Choy and Ya Choy.

SOURCES: Tsan and Ma International, P.O. Box 294, Belmont, California 94002; Kitazawa Seed Co., 356 W. Taylor St., San Jose, California 95110.

COOKING TIP 1
Obviously, Chinese cabbage can be used as you would domestic cabbage—i.e., raw in salads or stir-fried. But for a special treat, prepare a Chinese Lion's Head soup, so named because of the large meatballs it contains. Chinese cabbage is the most important and preponderant ingredient. This soup, by the way, is an excellent choice for a buffet dinner, for atop a fire in a chafing dish, the texture and consistency remains constant. Irene Kuo's *The Key to Chinese Cooking* contains an excellent recipe.

COOKING TIP 2
Last spring I gave some seeds of Chinese cabbage to my friends the Haralambou family, originally from Cyprus. They used the cabbage instead of grape leaves to wrap the classic Greek meat and rice—and found that the Chinese cabbage was much more tender than grape leaves.

Corn

SILVER QUEEN AND HONEY-
AND-CREAM VARIETIES

HARDINESS: Annual, tender.

WHEN TO PLANT: Sow after all danger of frost, from mid-May to early June, with successive plantings every 10 days.

SPACING: Rows 3 to 3 1/2 feet apart. Sow seeds 8 to 12 inches apart.

DEPTH: 1/2 inch.

HARVEST TIME: 78 to 92 days.

Truly an American triumph and as sacred to us as apple pie, Mom, and the Statue of Liberty. Surprisingly enough, Europeans are only beginning to appreciate our native vegetable. Oh, yes, you can purchase corn in the supermarkets—corn that may well be a week old. And rarely, if ever, can you get these two varieties, the white-kerneled Silver Queen and the yellow-and-white-colored Honey and Cream. If you don't live near farmers who grow these varieties and offer it for sale "just picked," grow your own. Corn must be eaten within a few hours after picking in order to be at its best. I start my pot boiling before I go out and pick the corn. Then I shuck it and put it right into the boiling water. Served with a little salt and pepper and dripping with butter, there's nothing quite like it.

HOW TO GROW SILVER QUEEN AND HONEY AND CREAM CORN

Cultivation is the same for these varieties as for everyday yellow corn. Plant in full sun after all danger of frost is past, mid-May to early June. Work a generous amount of rotted manure and compost into the soil, and just before planting the seed, work in handfuls of 5-10-5 fertilizer or organic mixture. Or dig a furrow 3 to 4 inches deep and put a band of 5-10-5 fertilizer or organic mixture into the furrow. Cover with soil, leaving a 1/2-inch-deep row for your seeds. Sow seeds 8 to 10 inches apart in rows about 3 feet apart.

No matter what shape and size your garden, keep in mind that corn must be pollinated, so plant two or three short rows of the vegetable rather than one long one in order to facilitate nature's work. Be sure to keep your crop weed-free, and as you hoe, build up the soil around the stalks for added support. Water generously during drought. When your corn kernels germinate, they will virtually explode with growth. So when the stalks are 6 to 12 inches high, fertilize again with 5-10-5 fertilizer (about 2 pounds per 100-foot row) or organic mix (about 4 pounds per 100-foot row).

Knowing when to harvest your corn is perhaps the key to good eating. If the ears ripen beyond the milky stage, the ears will be tough. To test the corn, gently press the sides of the ear. If the corn is ready to eat, it will feel firm and full to the touch. Then look at the silk on the end of the ear. It should be dry and of a rusty or even black color. To pick the ear, merely grasp it near the base and twist downward. It will separate from the stalk.

GARDENER'S TIP 1

Once the stalks have been totally stripped of ears, bend the stalks to the ground and cut them off at the base. By so doing, you will conserve nutrients in the soil.

GARDENER'S TIP 2

Do not let stalks stay in the ground over the winter. Once the crop has been harvested, pull the stalks from the ground and dispose of them or shred them and add to your compost heap. This helps control the corn borer.

GARDENER'S TIP 3
The long tight husks of Honey and Cream corn have some tendency to protect the ear from corn ear worms and other pests. It is a very sensible variety to grow.

PESTS: Corn earworms are green, brown, or pink with light stripes along their sides and backs. They are about 1 3/4 inches long when fully grown. If the silk of your corn looks as if it has been chewed and if kernels are damaged at the tip of the ear, your problem is earworms. As a preventative, simply place two or three drops of mineral oil into each ear of corn when the silk first appears. European corn borers are white, pink, or brown with a dark brown head; they grow up to 1 inch and are found in the stems. If the tassels are broken, or if a sawdustlike substance appears at the leaf axis, you probably have borers; cut and burn or bury the stalks immediately after harvest.

VARIETIES: Cream, Honey and Silver Queen.

SOURCE: W. Atlee Burpee Company, Warminster, Pennsylvania 18964, or Clinton, Iowa 52732.

COOKING TIP 1
Pick and boil immediately. That's it.

Cornichons

GHERKIN PICKLES

*

HARDINESS: Annual, tender.

WHEN TO PLANT: After all danger of frost, from mid-May to early June.

SPACING: In 1-foot-wide hills, spaced 2 1/2 feet apart. Plant five to seven seeds per hill.

DEPTH: 1/2 inch.

HARVEST TIME: About 60 days.

These are the tiny gherkin pickles which are served with pâtés and lemon wedges on the Continent. They are available in the markets, usually imported and quite expensive. You can grow them as easily as you grow domestic cucumbers and put them up yourself. They make very attractive gifts to give to friends at Christmas time, and they'll taste better than any you can buy.

HOW TO GROW CORNICHONS

Plant in full sun, in mid-May or early June, when all danger of frost is past. All cucumbers prefer a fertile, light, well-drained soil, so add well-rotted manure or organic matter to your cucumber hills. Also add side dressings of 5-10-5 fertilizer or organic mixture once the plants have started to grow. Mound up your soil to a height of about 6 inches and a width of about 1 foot. Plant from five to seven seeds in a small circle around the center of the hill. When seeds have germinated, thin to from three to five seedlings per hill. Keep well watered during the season, as cucumbers thrive on plenty of water.

If garden space is at a premium, you can grow cornichons in a row, if you provide netting or wire fence as support. Simply train the runners up the support. You will not need to support individual fruits with slings, as they are small. When the fruit begins to develop, check your crop each day, as all cucumbers grow very fast. Pick these when they are no longer than 1 1/2 inches in length for best results.

GARDENER'S TIP 1

A mulch beneath your cornichon patch will help to conserve water and keep your vegetables from contact with the soil, which will cause them to be green on one side and yellow on the other. Black plastic, grass clippings, or salt hay will help to conserve water, warm the soil, and impede rot.

GARDENER'S TIP 2

Remember to pick these every day, for once overgrown fruit appears on the vines, the plant will stop producing.

PESTS: Striped cucumber beetles are your main enemy. They are yellow to black in color with three black stripes down their backs. They grow to be about 1/5 inch long and feed on leaves, stems, and fruit. Hand-pick the beetles or use rotenone spray (5 table-spoons to 1 gallon water) or 1 percent rotenone dust. Squash vine borers, which are white and up to 1 inch long, can also be con-trolled to a certain extent with rotenone. The usual control, how-ever, is to slit the stem with a knife when the borer is located and to cover the leaf nodes with soil to induce rooting all along the stem. Squash bugs are brown with flat backs. Colonies are usually visible. In the evening lay down some boards near the plants. In the morning, lift up the boards and collect the gathered bugs.

VARIETY: West India Gherkin.

SOURCE: W. Atlee Burpee Co., Warminster, Pennsylvania 18964, or Clinton, Iowa 52732.

COOKING TIP 1

Several excellent recipes for pickling gherkins appear in *Larousse Gastronomique*. You will find that recipes calling for uncooked gherkins will result in a more crisp, fresher-tasting little pickle.

COOKING TIP 2

Helen Witty and Elizabeth Colchie's *Better Than Store-Bought* has a recipe for cornichon that I have found infallible.

COOKING TIP 3

As a quick substitute for cold pâté, use cold meatloaf. Serve very cold with gherkin pickles and slices of lemon. Your guests will never guess that it's leftover meatloaf. Surprisingly enough, the French love American meatloaf. They do not prepare it at home, and can't seem to get enough of the stuff. My friend Sue Blair, while living in Paris, always served cold meatloaf at her summer dinner parties. With the gherkins and lemon slices, it was a smashing success. In fact, she has become so famous for her meatloaf that in a recent book about the world of Paris high fashion, the chapter about her was entitled "Meatloaf Again."

Cress

DANISH CRESS

HARDINESS: Annual, very hardy.

WHEN TO PLANT: In early spring when ground is workable, then successively every 2 weeks throughout the summer.

SPACING: Rows about 1 foot apart; plant seeds thinly.

DEPTH: 1/4 inch.

HARVEST TIME: About 10 days after planting.

This is a peppery cousin of watercress, easily grown, that you can even cultivate indoors on a bed of cotton or felt. It's zesty tang brings springtime right to your table. And it is a splendid substitute for the water-grown variety (which, incidentally, you can grow at home, but it is a rather complicated process).

HOW TO GROW DANISH CRESS
Plant in full sun or semishade as soon as ground is workable and then about every 2 weeks for a continuous supply of young leaves. Sow the tiny seeds rather thinly, about 1/4 inch deep. To facilitate this, mix the seeds with sand before sowing. Cover with fine soil and keep moist until seeds germinate. You should be able to start picking in about 10 days. Plant successive crops every 2 weeks.

GARDENER'S TIP 1

At the end of the season, be sure to let some of your cress go to seed so that you will have a supply for the following season. Store seeds over the winter in a cool, dry, dark place.

PESTS: There are none.

VARIETIES: Burpee's Curlycress Salad Cress.

SOURCES: W. Atlee Burpee Co., Warminster, Pennsylvania 18964, or Clinton, Iowa 52732.

COOKING TIP 1

Tiny finger-size tea sandwiches are a great favorite in England and on the Continent. Cress is ideally suited for these. Simply take thinly sliced white bread, remove the crusts, butter lightly, and fill with peppery cress.

Eggplant

WHITE EGGPLANT OR
JAPANESE EGGPLANT

HARDINESS: Annual, tender.

WHEN TO PLANT: Since eggplant needs a long growing season, start plants indoors about 8 weeks before planting season, which is mid-May to early June.

SPACING: Indoors: 1/2 inch apart; outdoors: Plant seedlings 2 feet apart in rows 2 feet apart.

DEPTH: Indoors: 1/2 inch; outdoors: At soil line of plant.

HARVEST TIME: Anywhere from 100 to 140 days after sowing.

These smaller, more tender, and delicately flavored cousins of our own domestically grown purple variety will make an eggplant addict out of anyone with the slightest preference for this vegetable. And these are no more difficult to grow than our domestic eggplants.

HOW TO GROW WHITE EGGPLANT

Since a long growing season is necessary to ripen this vegetable, start indoors about 8 weeks before you plant tomatoes and peppers outside in your area. Plant the seeds 1/2 inch deep in containers. On top of 2 inches of potting or garden soil, spread about 1/2 inch of vermiculite or sphagnum moss. Then plant the eggplant seeds about 1/2 inch deep. Water thoroughly and cover the containers. As the plants grow, transplant them to separate containers such as peat pots or cut-off milk cartons and fill with a good garden loam. Place your plants in a south window and keep well watered. After about 6 weeks, begin to harden the plants off by placing them outside on warm, sunny days. Then about 1 week before planting, leave the plants out overnight *if* the temperature is not too cold. The following week transplant them into the garden in a spot that receives full sun. But be sure to select a gray day, as the hot sun may burn and wilt the young seedlings.

Your soil should be rich, so fortify with several wheelbarrow loads of manure or rotted compost per 50-foot row. Also add about 5 pounds of 5-10-5 fertilizer or 10 pounds of organic mixture to each row.

Dig shallow holes about 2 feet apart for your plants and fill them with water. When the water has settled in, place your plants in the soil and fill up the hole with soil.

Be sure to fashion collars of aluminum foil, cardboard, or tin cans to place around your plants when you set them in. These will ward off cutworms. Firm the soil around the roots. This will leave a slight depression, which will serve to catch water. If during the next day or so the sun is inordinately strong and the plants wilt, simply water well and provide some sort of temporary shade for them. Control weeds during the season and water thoroughly during drought. Harvest these eggplants when they are only 2 inches in diameter.

GARDENER'S TIP 1

Chances are your plants will set more fruit than the plant can reasonably produce. When the initial blossoms have set and fruit begins to form, pinch off all later blossoms. In that way, your plants will produce vegetables of quality rather than in great numbers.

GARDENER'S TIP 2

To avoid weeding, lay down a mulch of black plastic, grass clippings, or salt hay.

GARDENER'S TIP 3

Out here where I live on the far eastern end of Long Island, the farmers grow potatoes, hence the Colorado potato beetle is quite prolific. Eggplant attracts them, so if you are not prepared to hand-pick the beetles or spray with rotenone, avoid this crop.

PESTS: To avoid blossom-end rot, those dark, sunken leathery spots at the end of the fruits, water well during the early growing stages. Leaf miners can be controlled with 25 percent Diazinon EC, but keep in mind that this chemical is toxic.

VARIETIES: Japanese Eggplant or White Eggplant.

SOURCES: Tsang and Ma International, P.O. Box 294, Belmont, California 94002; Kitazawa Seed Co., 356 W. Taylor St., San Jose, California 95110.

COOKING TIP 1
Here's an easy way to prepare this vegetable when you are barbecueing teriyaki steak or chicken. Simply cook the entire unpeeled eggplant alongside. Use slow burning coals and cook until soft, about 10 minutes on each side. Serve with grated daikon (see page 84) or grated ginger root and soy sauce.

Escarole

ALSO CALLED ENDIVE
IN THE UNITED STATES

HARDINESS: Annual, very hardy.

WHEN TO PLANT: In early spring, as soon as ground can be worked.

SPACING: Rows about 1 foot apart. Plant seeds 1/2 inch apart and thin as season progresses to about 8 inches apart. Successive plantings every 10 days or so will ensure a summer-long supply.

DEPTH: 1/2 inch.

HARVEST TIME: Anywhere from 3 to 7 weeks (3 weeks for first thinning to 7 weeks before bolting).

Escarole is the correct name for this vegetable. In this country it is often called endive, a far cry from the Belgian endive which we call witloof. You get points if you can figure that all out. Escarole is grown in the same manner as lettuce, and is very useful in mixed salads, adding distinctive taste.

HOW TO GROW ESCAROLE

Plant in late March or early April as soon as the ground is workable. Escarole likes full sun, abundant moisture, and a reasonably fertile soil, so fortify with compost, rotted manure, and handfuls of 5-10-5 fertilizer or organic mixture spread along the rows. Sow the seeds thinly about 1/2 inch deep, cover with soil, tamp down, and keep moist. After about 3 weeks you can start to thin out your escarole, adding the tiny leaves to salads. Continue to thin out as the season progresses until the heads stand about 8 inches apart. Plant successive crops every 10 days or so until the heat of summer. Escarole will bolt in heat, making it bitter and inedible.

Plant again in early September for a fall crop.

GARDENER'S TIP 1
Beware of rabbits. Plant escarole in a fenced area.

PESTS: Escarole is relatively pest-free.

VARIETIES: Green Curled, Broad-Leafed Batavian

SOURCE: W. Atlee Burpee Co., Warminster, Pennsylvania 18974, or Clinton, Iowa 52732.

COOKING TIP 1
If you plant a fall crop of escarole you can cut the heads after the first frost; tie the outer leaves around the heads to blanch the centers, and store them in a cool, dark place. The vegetable will keep that way for as long as a month. Escarole adapts very well to soup recipes calling for chicory or endive. A cream of escarole soup recipe worth investigating appears in the *Larousse Gastronomique.*

Finocchio

FLORENCE FENNEL

HARDINESS: Annual, tender.

WHEN TO PLANT: After all danger of frost, from mid-May to early June.

SPACING: In rows 1 1/2 feet apart, sow seeds about 1/2 inch apart, thinning to about 8 inches.

DEPTH: About 1/2 inch.

HARVEST TIME: Leaves can be picked in midseason, stalks later on, and seeds in late fall.

Surely one of the most versatile of vegetables, fennel leaves impart a delicate anise flavor to soups, salads, fish, and eggs. The stalks are delicious when mature, and the dried seeds collected in the fall can be used in confections and baked goods. Rarely available in markets, except perhaps in Italian neighborhoods, finocchio is easily grown in your garden.

HOW TO GROW FINOCCHIO
When you plant your beans, it is time to plant finocchio, that is, in mid-May or early June. Fortify the soil with rotted manure, compost, and 5-10-5 fertilizer or organic mixture and plant in full sun. Plant seeds about 1/2 inch apart, 1/2 inch deep, and when

seedlings are 3 inches high, thin to 8 inches. Cultivate and water throughout the season. After about 2 months, some of the leaves can be removed from each plant for use in salads or soups. Then in September, when the stalks are broad and white, they can be used as a prepared vegetable. Let some plants go to seed in the late fall. Collect the seeds and use them in sweets or when you bake rolls or bread. Be sure to save some for planting next season.

GARDENER'S TIP 1
The strong anise odor of finocchio repels many insects from other vegetables.

PESTS: Finocchio is pest-free.

VARIETY: Florence Fennel.

SOURCE: W. Atlee Burpee Co., Warminster, Pennsylvania 18974, or Clinton, Iowa 52732.

COOKING TIP 1
Mediterranean people all enjoy finocchio. The Italians first parboil the stalks in water and then sauté them in butter, adding grated Parmesan cheese when they are done. The vegetable is often served with roast pork with bay leaves. See Marcella Hazan's *The Classic Italian Cook Book* for a traditional recipe. The Greeks use finocchio in salads, mixing it with olives, feta cheese, onions, and lettuce.

COOKING TIP 2
A delicious sauce for fish or white meat can be made with finocchio and parsley, along with other ingredients. See *The Nouvelle Cuisine of Jean & Pierre Troisgros* for an appetizing recipe.

Garlic, Elephant

HARDINESS: Annual or biennial, very hardy.

WHEN TO PLANT: In early spring when ground is workable or in the fall with winter protection.

SPACING: Rows 1 foot apart. Plant sets 6 inches apart.

DEPTH: With pointed tops about 1/2 inch below surface of soil.

HARVEST TIME: Late August, early September.

Giant elephant garlic is a recent addition to the gourmet vegetable scene. The taste is just a shade sweeter than conventional garlic, but the size is monumental. Under proper conditions elephant garlic grows to the size of a man's fist.

HOW TO GROW ELEPHANT GARLIC

To achieve the gigantic size, you must plant the cloves in the fall. Then, protect through the winter with a hefty covering of mulch leaves and mounded earth. Plant the cloves blunt side down, about 6 inches apart, with the tops about 1/2 inch below the surface of the soil. Space your rows 1 foot apart. Be sure to select a spot in the garden that receives full sun. Fortify the soil with plenty of compost, rotted manure, and some 5-10-5 fertilizer or organic mixture. The following spring, remove your winter covering and cultivate to assure a weed-free patch. In late August or early September, when the leaves have turned brown, dig the garlic and place the bulbs on a screen in the sun to dry. Be sure there is adequate ventilation during this period. The following week, cut off the tops, rub the dead leaves, skin, and dry soil off the bulbs, and store them in a cool, dry place. Each garlic bulb will produce about one dozen cloves.

GARDENER'S TIP 1
You can plant elephant garlic in the spring, at the same time that you plant onions and shallots, but the bulbs will not grow to full size. If you choose to do this, follow cultivation instructions for shallots.

GARDENER'S TIP 2
As with shallots, be sure to save some cloves from your fall crop. Either plant them in the fall or save for the spring.

GARDENER'S TIP 3
If you plant a great deal of garlic in your garden, you will have little trouble with insect pests.

PESTS: There are none.

VARIETY: Elephant Garlic.

SOURCE: J. A. Demonchaux Co., 225 Jackson, Topeka, Kansas 66603.

COOKING TIP 1

As you know, if you love garlic, you'll try to put it in everything you eat. Here's a suggestion for garlic lovers. If you've traveled in the Mexican countryside, you've undoubtedly sampled their garlic soup. It's easily prepared at home. Just heat about 1 quart chicken broth, add 2 minced garlic cloves, a dash of salt, and some freshly ground black pepper; simmer for about 10 minutes. Pour boiling hot soup into warmed bowls at the table and break a fresh egg into each bowl of soup. The egg will poach right in the bowl.

Ginger Root

HARDINESS: Very tender; grow as houseplant.

Those who enjoy Chinese or Indian cuisine know that fresh ginger root is a basic spice. You can grow it in a pot in your house. It's easily raised and makes a fine addition to your houseplant collection. If you decide to grow ginger root, you will not only have a free, steady supply of this spice but a handsome plant and, if you're lucky, flowers as well.

HOW TO GROW GINGER ROOT

To grow ginger root, buy one in the market. The root is a gnarled, knobby rhizome, brown outside and pale yellow inside. This is what you plant and ultimately use in cooking. Choose a healthy specimen, one that is firm and plump with a shiny skin. Soft wrinkled ginger roots will rot in a pot.

To plant the root, fill a 6-inch container with a mixture of one part potting soil, two parts sand, and one part humus or peat moss. Be sure to place gravel or flower pot shards in the bottom of the container for drainage. Bury the ginger root just below the soil surface and thoroughly soak the container with warm water.

Place the pot in a south window or, barring that, a west window. If you have only eastern or northern exposure in your house or apartment, grow ginger plants under lights, as they need plenty of sunshine. If the house or apartment is dry in the winter, spray mist daily. Keep your plant evenly moist throughout the growing season.

In several weeks, green shoots will emerge, growing ultimately to a height of about 2 1/2 to 3 feet. Leaves of the plant are elongated and are placed alternately on the stem, arranged in two vertical rows. Your plant may have to be staked at this point.

If conditions are ideal—that is, if the plant receives enough light and moisture—the ginger plant may flower. Blooms are borne on leafless stems from 6 to 12 inches high and are formed in dense conelike spikes. The spikes are about 1 inch thick and from 2 to 3 inches long, composed of overlapping green bracts which may be edged in yellow. Each bract encloses a small yellow-green and purple flower.

Now for the harvest. When the roots have completely filled the container—that is, when the plant is potbound and roots are seen emerging from the drainage holes at the bottom of the container—it is time to harvest. Unpot the plant, shake the dirt off, and wash the roots. Cut off a 2- or 3-inch part of the new root system to start another crop. Discard the original part of the root which was planted.

To store ginger root, either keep it in a dry, cool place, freeze, or place in an airtight container, cover it with sherry wine, and store in the refrigerator. It will keep indefinitely. You will not

need much of this spice to prepare exotic dishes, as ginger is strong and peppery.

PESTS: There are none.

VARIETY: Simply ginger root.

SOURCE: Your local supermarket or Oriental specialty shop.

COOKING TIP 1
Ginger root is as basic to Oriental cooking as salt and pepper is to Western cuisine. However, there are some Chinese and Japanese fish dishes which include a spicy ginger and scallion sauce. An excellent recipe can be found in Irene Kuo's *The Key to Chinese Cooking.*

Haricots Verts

FRENCH BUSH GREEN BEANS

HARDINESS: Annual, tender.

WHEN TO PLANT: After all danger of frost from mid-May to early June, as bean seeds react badly to cool, damp conditions. Then, every 2 weeks for successive crops.

SPACING: Rows about 2 feet apart. Plant seeds about 2 to 3 inches apart.

DEPTH: About 1 inch.

HARVEST TIME: 45 to 55 days after planting.

In France, there is no such thing as French-cut beans—the bean shredder or slicer, as we know it, is unknown. The reason is that an entirely different kind of bean from the American variety is grown and favored. And with good reason, for the haricots verts *(filets)* are very thin, delicate vegetables. To put it simply, they taste better than ours. In this country, they occasionally appear on menus of elegant hotels or restaurants, but generally are imported from France and thus are astronomical in price. Ten dollars for a small side dish is not unusual. You can have them on your table all summer long and, if you freeze your surplus, during the winter as well, for there is absolutely no trick to growing them. If you have grown such domestic varieties of snap beans such as

Tender Pod or Top Crop, you can grow these—the culture is exactly the same. The two things that you must know to grow them is a source of the seed, and when to harvest the beans.

HOW TO GROW HARICOTS VERTS

Beans require full sun and will grow well in any moderately fertile soil. Generally, heavy feeding is not necessary, although a side dressing of 5-10-5 or organic mixture won't hurt. With a hoe, make a row 1 to 2 inches in depth and plant the seeds 2 to 3 inches apart. Cover with soil and tamp down. Cultivate to keep free of weeds throughout the growing season and keep well watered during droughts. About 6 weeks later you will notice scores of very thin string beans developing on the bushes.

GARDENER'S TIP 1

Rabbits relish small bean plants, so unless you take precautions, you may have little left for yourself. They must be enclosed by a fence.

GARDENER'S TIP 2

The secret to harvesting these beans is to pick them when they are very young. Do not wait for them to grow to the thickness of domestic varieties. They should measure perhaps 1/4 inch across and 4 inches in length. Try to pick your beans every day, for your plants will produce more beans if you do. Do not wait for them to grow to the size of domestic beans.

GARDENER'S TIP 3

There is an old maxim that states: do not cultivate haricots verts when the morning dew is on them. I experimented and found that, yes, the maxim is true. Bean rust *is* easily spread at that time.

GARDENER'S TIP 4

Inoculate your bean seeds before planting, if you haven't grown beans successfully there before. Simply purchase some inoculant from your garden center and proceed as follows. Moisten the seed, pour on the powder, roll the seed in the powder, coating it generously, and plant the seed. The inoculant is a bacteria powder that helps the plant do its job of taking nitrogen from the air and storing it in the plant's root nodules.

PESTS: Mexican bean beetles and bean leaf beetles are the only pests. Both can be controlled with a 5 percent rotenone WP (5 tablespoons to 1 gallon of water).

VARIETIES: Fin de Bagnols, Roi Belges, Triomphe de Farcy, and a new addition, Radar. The advantage of Radar is that the beans are borne higher up on the plant, producing a cleaner vegetable and one easier to pick.

SOURCE: J. A. Demonchaux Co., 827 North Kansas, Topeka, Kansas 66608.

COOKING TIP 1

Avoid doing exotic things to these choice morsels. Simply boil or steam them and serve with butter. If you can avoid salt, do so, as the delicate flavor of these beans will be more readily savored.

COOKING TIP 2

M. Dominique Ferriere, the chef at the very elegant Chateau du Domaine de St. Martin, in the charming town of Vence, near Nice, suggests this method of cooking these delectables:

Fill a very large pot with water, add salt, and bring to a rapid boil. Then pour in the haricots verts and boil rapidly uncovered. When the beans are *al dente,* that is crisp to the bite, about 8 to 10 minutes, remove them and plunge them in ice water.

COOKING TIP 3

At the PLM Ile Rousse in Bandol, also in the south of France, chef Luc Grillot cuts the beans into half-inch lengths, cooks them *al dente,* and marinates them in oil, vinegar, and shallots—a simple but elegant accompaniment to a summer lunch or dinner.

Horseradish

HARDINESS: Perennial, hardy.

WHEN TO PLANT: In early spring as soon as ground is workable.

SPACING: Rows 1 foot apart, root cuttings 1 to 2 feet apart.

DEPTH: To soil line on plants, usually between root and crown.

HARVEST TIME: From spring through fall as needed, but spring diggings are best.

Why settle for the bottled variety, when home-grown horseradish is infinitely more pungent and tasty? There are no tricks to growing horseradish, and it is virtually indestructible.

HOW TO GROW HORSERADISH
Either purchase stock from a garden center or mail order nursery or purchase a root in the market and cut it into root cuttings. To do this, cut the root into pieces 6 to 8 inches long, the thickness of a lead pencil, and plant in full sun. Horseradish can also be propagated from crown cuttings. Merely cut a piece of the root and crown bud from a specimen and plant. Spring is the best time to do this. Dig a trench 4 to 5 inches deep and place the cuttings at an angle with their tops near the surface of the ground. Usually

new roots will develop during the first year. Once established, pieces of roots and crowns remaining in the soil after harvest are usually sufficient to reestablish the plants.

GARDENER'S TIP 1
Since horseradish is a perennial plant, select a site in your garden away from the annual Rototilling. Also, be sure to keep the plants in check, as horseradish can be invasive, spreading rampantly.

PESTS: There are none.

VARIETIES: Simply New Bohemian Horseradish.

SOURCE: Most mail order nurseries and many local garden centers.

COOKING TIP 1
Horseradish sauces are served as accompaniment to many meats and fish. Combine it with whipped cream and serve with smoked fish or boiled beef.

COOKING TIP 2
Although grated horseradish combined with grated beets is a standard condiment in Eastern Europe, most Americans have never tasted it. It is served with traditional Easter hunt breakfasts in Poland and Russia and is easily prepared: combine 1/2 cup grated horseradish with 1 cup grated cooked beets, 4 tablespoons white vinegar, 1 tablespoon sugar, and 1 teaspoon salt. Store in the refrigerator. It will keep for about 1 month. It is excellent with hard-boiled eggs and cold smoked ham.

Kipfel Kartoffel

FINGERLING OR
LADY FINGER POTATOES

✑

HARDINESS: Annual, hardy.

WHEN TO PLANT: Between the end of March and April 15, when the soil is friable and not too muddy. Later in the far northern reaches of the country.

SPACING: About 1 1/2 feet apart.

DEPTH: 6 to 8 inches.

HARVEST TIME: Late summer.

These diminutive yellow-fleshed potatoes are well known to gardeners and gourmets throughout Europe. They grow about 1 inch in diameter, several inches long, and have a flavor and quality all their own. They are not porous or mealy in texture as common table potatoes, but waxy and firm, producing a potato salad unexcelled. Today Kipfel Kartoffel are grown commercially in Austria, but because the local demand is so great, exporting seed potatoes is against the law. In other words, the only way you can eat these in the United States is if you grow them yourself. They require a little more effort than most crops, but are indeed worth the time.

HOW TO GROW KIPFEL KARTOFFELS

Several days before planting time mix together about 4 gallons of rotted manure, compost, and 2 pounds of 5-10-5 fertilizer or 4 pounds of organic mixture and spread it over a 5-by-10-foot plot. This size plot will ultimately provide you with about half a bushel of potatoes. Plant in full sun. Dig the mixture into the soil to a depth of 10 inches. Several days later, dig furrows 6 to 8 inches deep, in rows about 1 1/2 feet apart. Plant the seed potatoes whole and cover them gently with soil.

When they have grown about 6 to 8 inches high, usually around 3 weeks later, hill the soil around the stems as high as the lower leaves (about 6 inches). Then 2 to 3 weeks later, when they have grown another 6 or 8 inches, hill them again to the lower leaves. Cultivate your crop during the summer or mulch with grass clipping, straw, or other material but do *not* water them. Kipfel Kartoffels do not have the water content of domestic potatoes. In other words, the firmer they are, the better they are.

In the fall, when the tops of the plants have become brown and start to wilt and when the soil is dry, dig the potatoes. Do not dig them after rain or when the soil is muddy. Do not be disappointed at low yield. Kipfel Kartoffel plants produce about 20 to 25 percent of the regular potato yield.

Dry the potatoes for a few hours in the shade. *Never put them in the sun.* Do not wash the crop, as water causes rapid deterioration of quality.

Store your crop in a cool, dry, dark place, in a bushel basket covered with newspaper. A cellar or unheated garage is suitable. When the deep freeze of winter arrives, store them in a place where they will not freeze. They should keep through the winter.

GARDENER'S TIP 1

Although it is not supposed to work, I did it successfully. Simply store a supply of the potatoes in the refrigerator over the winter and then plant them in the spring.

GARDENER'S TIP 2

Remember not to expose your potatoes to the sun after you've dug them. Although the released poison won't kill you, it will make you quite ill. This, incidentally, is true of all potatoes, for they are members of the nightshade family.

PESTS: Colorado potato beetles may well attack your plants. They are yellow with black stripes on their wing segments. Either hand-pick them off or spray with 5 percent rotenone WP, 5 tablespoons of rotenone to 1 gallon of water.

VARIETY: Ladyfinger, Yellow Finger, or Kipfel Kartoffel.

SOURCE: Gurney Seed Company, Yankton, South Dakota 57079. This is the only source I know of in the United States. One pound should be enough to plant a 5-by-10 plot.

COOKING TIP 1

When cooking these potatoes for eating, boil them with the skins on. I have found that if you cut them in half before boiling, you simply squeeze them and the delectable waxy, yellow potatoes come right out of their skins. Kipfel Kartoffels can be eaten in salad or fried as hash browns. But they are not suitable for mashing, French frying, or baking.

COOKING TIP 2

Probably the best potato salad on earth is made from these potatoes. Here's the recipe. Boil about 4 cups of Kipfel Kartoffels as you would the common kitchen potato. After about 15 minutes, test one of the larger potatoes with a cake tester. If it goes in without any difficulty, your potatoes are done. To make potato salad, prepare while the potatoes are still warm. You will notice that they are firm, not porous like common potatoes. For this reason, oils, vinegar, or mayonnaise will not be absorbed if they are cold. The 4 cups of potatoes should yield about 2 cups sliced. Put them in a bowl and add 1 teaspoon minced onion, 2 tablespoons peanut oil, and about 1 teaspoon white vinegar. Salt and pepper to taste. You can also add some chopped parsley, hard-boiled egg, and/or bacon bits if you like. Mix this together and chill to the bone in the refrigerator. I have made the traditional American potato salad with mayonnaise, using these potatoes, but found their delicate flavor overpowered by the mayonnaise.

Leeks

HARDINESS: Annual, hardy.

WHEN TO PLANT: In early spring, as soon as ground is workable.

SPACING: Rows 2 feet apart. Thin plants to 4 to 6 inches apart.

DEPTH: 1/2 inch.

HARVEST TIME: 4 to 6 months.

Ah, the mighty leek. A joy to the palate but expensive and difficult to find in the markets. There is a little more work involved in growing this superb vegetable than most, but well worth the time and effort.

HOW TO GROW LEEKS
You can produce a healthy leek crop in any soil that is neutral or nonacid with good drainage. Full sun is required, along with sufficient moisture and weed-free conditions.

There are two ways to grow this vegetable. You can either start seeds indoors about 6 weeks before early spring planting or sow them directly in the soil at the earliest moment you can dig. The reason for starting indoors is that leeks require a growing season of some 130 days to reach maturity. If you want fresh leeks by the end of summer, you will have to start seeds indoors. If you are willing to wait until late fall, plant seeds directly outdoors later. One advantage of late planting is that with a minimum of protection, leeks will winter over, and in the spring, as soon as the soil thaws out, you can dig fresh leeks for your table.

If you plan on starting seeds indoors, simply plant them 1/2 inch deep in your planting medium. Place the trays in a sunny window and 6 weeks later, when the plants have reached a height of from 6 to 8 inches, transplant into the garden.

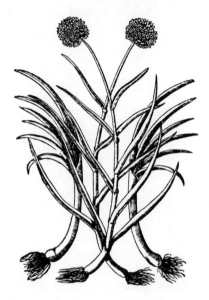

Prepare the soil for your bed by adding rotted manure or compost. A scattering of 5-10-5 fertilizer or organic mixture should be worked in as well. Be sure to rake out stones and other debris, as leeks must grow in friable soil in order to form properly. If you are planting seeds directly into the garden, sow them about 1/2 inch deep. When they are 6 to 8 inches tall, transplant them to another row, following instructions below for seedlings started indoors.

When your seedlings are 6 weeks old and ready for trans-plant, dig them and snip off half of the upper leaf portion. Then dig a furrow about 6 to 8 inches deep. Plant the leeks 4 to 6 inches apart and cover only to the soil line. As the leeks grow, fill in the furrow with soil. This will serve to blanch the bottom, edible root portion of the plants. About 3 1/2 months later, when the leek is of considerable size, pull one to see if it is ready for the table. It should resemble a monumental scallion.

GARDENER'S TIP 1

Mulching is a difficult task for leeks—since you mound your rows with dirt to blanch, it is nearly impossible to keep the mulch in place. Cultivate frequently and remove other weeds by hand picking.

GARDENER'S TIP 2

Be sure to leave some of your crop in the ground over the winter. Pile dead leaves or compost over the plants, then after the spring thaw, dig them up for a special early spring treat. You can also winter them over in a cold frame if you wish.

GARDENER'S TIP 3

Leeks need watering during drought periods. Be sure to give them at least 1 1/2 inches of water a week.

PESTS: Generally leeks, like other members of the onion family, are pest-free. If onion maggots strike, use 57 percent Malathion EC (2 teaspoons to 1 gallon of water). These worms bore into the bulbs, causing them to shrivel. Thrips are yellow to brown, winged, very active, and about 1/25 inch long. They cause white blotches to appear on the leaves, which eventually wither and die. The same Malathion solution will arrest the destruction. Be sure to follow instructions for using this chemical to the letter. There are some hazards involved in its use.

VARIETY: Broad London is the most widely planted.

SOURCE: Most mail order seed houses and local garden centers carry a supply of leek seeds. Leek sets are available from Le Jardin du Gourmet, West Danville, Vermont 05873. By ordering sets, you won't have to start seeds indoors or transplant your outdoor sown seedlings.

COOKING TIP 1

For a very elegant fish course, prepare a basic fish mousse mixture out of about 1 pound of sole or flounder fillets. Then cut the base off of 3 leeks and separate the leaves. Wash 12 or 14 of the largest leaves and parboil for about 6 minutes. Trim leek leaves into rectangles about 9 inches long, place about 3 tablespoons of the uncooked mousse on each, and roll into tidy pockets. Place the pockets seam down in a buttered baking pan, 8 inches by 14 inches, along with 5 tablespoons clam juice. Dot with butter, cover with aluminum foil, and bring to a boil on the range. Then bake in a preheated 400-degree oven for 15 minutes. Serve immediately with a beurre blanc sauce.

Lettuce

GOURMET VARIETIES

HARDINESS: Annual, hardy.

WHEN TO PLANT: In early spring, as soon as ground is workable.

SPACING: In rows about 1 foot apart, sow seeds 1/2 inch apart and thin as the season progresses to about 8 inches apart.

DEPTH: 1/2 inch.

HARVEST TIME: From 3 to 10 weeks—3 weeks for first thinning, 10 weeks before bolting.

You've probably long since tired of our American iceberg lettuce, and know about romaine and Bibb lettuce, sometimes available in the markets. But there are dozens of delectable varieties of lettuce which are available only from your own garden. American varieties such as Buttercrunch, Green Ice, Black-Seeded Simpson, and Salad Bowl are all excellent, but beyond that there are French varieties which are even more tempting. All lettuce is easily grown, relatively pest-free, and a treat in the salad bowl. And, to make this very utilitarian vegetable even more tempting, there are three basic types of lettuce. First there is head lettuce, which grows in tight little heads; leaf lettuce, which produces crisp, crinkly, or curly-leafed specimens; and cos or romaine lettuce,

63

which develops tightly folded leaves that grow in an upright manner.

HOW TO GROW GOURMET LETTUCE

Plant as soon as ground is workable in the spring. Lettuce prefers full sun, abundant moisture, and a reasonably fertile soil, so fortify with compost, rotted manure, and a sprinkling of 5-10-5 fertilizer or organic mixture. Sow seeds thinly, about 1/2 inch deep, and cover with soil. Tamp down and keep moist until seeds germinate. Plan on planting successive crops every 10 days or so in order to ensure a longer season. After several weeks you will be able to start thinning your lettuce bed, enjoying the plants you pull in salad. Continue to thin heading and cos varieties until plants stand about 8 inches apart. Leaf lettuce can stand about 6 inches apart. Lettuce bolts and turns bitter during the heat of high summer. When cool weather returns in early September, plant a fall crop.

GARDENER'S TIP 1

This is gourmet food for rabbits, so be sure to fence in your lettuce patch.

GARDENER'S TIP 2

Part of the secret of extending the lettuce season well into the summer is to be sure that your bed is well watered almost daily during extreme hot or dry spells. It doesn't always work, but it is worth a try. You can also cover part of your crop with lattice to provide some shade.

GARDENER'S TIP 3

Since lettuce generally bolts by mid-July, interplanting with later fall vegetables or even tomatoes can conserve space.

GARDENER'S TIP 4

Do not pick lettuce before ten o'clock in the morning. Studies have proved that the leaves are higher in vitamin content after that hour. If your lettuce is not as crisp-looking later in the day, simply drench it in a pot of ice water. It will crisp up nicely.

PESTS: Cabbage loopers and aphids may be troublesome. Pick the loopers by hand and use a peppery spray from your garden hose to dislodge the aphids.

VARIETIES: Kagraner Sommer, heat-resistant; Marvel of Four Seasons, reddish outer leaves and blond inner leaves; Romaine Ballon, a cos lettuce resistant to heat; Summer White, a large head with blond leaves, very slow in bolting; and Winter Marvel, large-headed and especially good for fall planting, as it survives early autumn low temperatures.

SOURCE: J. A. Demonchaux Co., 827 North Kansas, Topeka, Kansas 66608.

COOKING TIP 1

Since your garden will provide plenty of lettuce for an extravagant dish of braised stuffed lettuces, *The Nouvelle Cuisine of Jean and Pierre Troisgros* offers a savory recipe for this treat.

Lily Buds

HARDINESS: Perennial

WHEN TO PLANT: From spring to summer.

SPACING: Set plants about 2 feet apart.

DEPTH: Soil level of plants.

HARVEST TIME: In late spring when buds form, before flowers open.

If you cook in the Chinese manner, you know that lily buds are an ingredient often used in the preparation of this cuisine. Growing your own is foolproof, as these plants are virtually indestructible. Cultivated varieties are called day lilies. You probably already have some in your garden, but were not aware that the buds are indeed edible and very delicious at that.

HOW TO GROW LILY BUDS

You can buy day lilies in your local nursery, order them from mail order houses, or simply dig a clump of the wild lilies. Plants should be divided into stock about 6 inches in diameter. Plant them at soil level, in full sun or partial shade, and forget about them. They are pest-free and maintenance-free, with an attractive growing habit and handsome foliage. In the late spring, pick the buds before they bloom and dry them. Simply tie together in bunches, then hang them upside down to dry in a cool, dry, shady place. When they are thoroughly dry, remove the buds from the stalks and store in airtight containers in a cool, dark, dry place.

PESTS: There are none.

VARIETIES: They come in many colors and make welcome, maintenance-free additions to your flower garden.

SOURCE: In the wild or day lilies from nurseries or mail order houses.

COOKING TIP 1
Dried lily buds are a basic ingredient in Chinese hot and sour soup and are often combined with cloud ear mushrooms in creating various meat and poultry dishes. They are also very good served raw or deep-fried as tempura.

Mâche

CORN SALAD OR
LAMB'S LETTUCE

HARDINESS: Annual, hardy.

WHEN TO PLANT: In early spring with successive plantings every few weeks.

SPACING: Rows about 1 foot apart, plant seeds 1/2 inch apart, and thin as season progresses to about 6 inches.

DEPTH: 1/2 inch.

HARVEST TIME: 3 to 6 weeks after planting and then throughout the summer.

Mâche, a salad green very popular in Europe, is generally eaten during the hot months of summer and early fall when lettuce is unavailable in the garden. Start thinning after 3 weeks and use leaves in salads.

HOW TO GROW MÂCHE
Plant in early spring and then every 2 weeks until fall. Several varieties are cold-resistant and will continue to flourish well into the cooler autumn months. Mâche likes full sun, firm soil, and plenty of moisture during the summer months. Sow seeds about 1/2 inch apart and 1/2 inch deep and thin to about 6 inches.

PESTS: Few, if any.

VARIETIES: Big Seed, Green Full Heart, Green Cambrai.

SOURCE: J. A. Demonchaux Co., 827 North Kansas, Topeka, Kansas 66608.

COOKING TIP 1

You've probably never eaten this vegetable, let alone cultivated it, but I urge you to try it. Fresh green salad material in the heat of summer is difficult to come by in your garden. Mâche will satisfy your needs. The Sheraton Hotel in Paris is famous for its summer mâche salad. The chef combines mâche with red leaf lettuce, endive, head lettuce, oil, Roquefort cheese, fresh cream, and cumin to taste. Not only does it taste good, but it is eye-appealing as well.

Melon Charantais

HARDINESS: Annual, tender.

WHEN TO PLANT: After all danger of frost, from mid-May to early June.

SPACING: 1 1/2-foot-wide hills spaced 3 feet apart. Plant five to seven seeds per hill.

DEPTH: 1/2 inch.

HARVEST TIME: 80 to 85 days.

Many American varieties of cantaloupe or muskmelon are truly superb in texture and flavor, but if you've ever traveled to France during high summer or early fall and sampled the superb Charantais variety, you probably remember it as the most delicious you've ever tasted. And then, if you grow your own melons, you can pick them vine-ripened. As you know from growing your own tomatoes, there is simply no comparison with the supermarket version. These melons are smaller than ours, so don't be dismayed if they don't look like domestic varieties. But wait until you taste them!

Up to now, there has been a small problem in their cultivation because varieties available in this country have not been resistant to fusarium wilt. Cantaloupe Ido was introduced last year and is resistant to the disease. You won't regret investing the little extra effort required to grow these choice melons.

HOW TO GROW CHARANTAIS MELONS

Plant in mid-May or early June when all danger of frost is past. Melons, like cucumbers and squash, are planted in small mounds measuring about 1 1/2 feet across. They prefer full sun. Dig a small hole about 6 inches deep and 1 foot across and fill it with rotted manure and compost. Then build up your hill to about 6 inches in height. Plant from five to seven seeds in a small circle around the center of the hill. When seeds have germinated, thin to from three to five seedlings per hill. Keep well watered during the season, as melons thrive on lots of water.

GARDENER'S TIP 1

In France, Charantais melons are pruned to produce a better-tasting and earlier-setting fruit. Here's how you do it: When the plant has two sets of leaves, that is the cotyledons (the first set which grows and not characteristic of the true leaves) and the first set of true leaves, remove the cotyledons. When the plant has grown two more leaves, pinch out the middle shoot. This will force the vines to grow out diagonally from the main stem. Then, when each of the two side vines have produced three or four leaves, pinch the end again. These side vines will then produce secondary vines which should be pinched in the center when they have produced two to four leaves. Finally, when the plant has set fruit, allow only three to four melons per plant to develop. You don't have to do this, but if you do your melons will be of superior quality.

GARDENER'S TIP 2

Most novices don't know when to pick melons. They are ripe when the stem separates easily from the vine. Just pick a melon up in your hand and move it around gently. If it separates from the vine, it is ripe and ready to pick. If not, wait a day or so and repeat the process until it does separate.

GARDENER'S TIP 3

If space is a problem, plant your melon seeds in a row and train them to grow up a fence or trellis. As the melons develop, fashion slings out of cloth and secure them to the fence.

GARDENER'S TIP 4
A mulch beneath your melon patch will help to conserve water
and keep your melons from contact with the soil, which may
impede ripening. Black plastic, grass clippings, or other mulch
materials will serve you well.

GARDENER'S TIP 5
Protect from rabbits, birds—and believe it or not, turtles! They'll
walk miles to taste your melons. In addition to the fence around
my garden, I also protect my melons with pieces of chicken wire
placed over individual specimens.

PESTS: As with cucumbers, striped cucumber beetles are your
main problem. They are yellow to black in color with three black
stripes down their backs and grow to about 1/5 inch long. They
feed on leaves, stems, and fruit. Hand-pick the beetles or use
rotenone spray (5 tablespoons to 1 gallon of water) or 1 percent
rotenone dust. Squash vine borers are white, up to 1 inch long,
and are also controlled with rotenone. Squash bugs are brown
with flat backs. You can spot colonies of these devils. At sun-
down, lay boards down near the plants. The bugs will spend the
night under the boards. Early in the morning, lift them up, collect,
and dispose of the bugs. Also, hoe soil over the leaf nodes to
induce additional rooting and counter the attacks of the vine
borers.

VARIETY: Cantaloupe Charantais, Cantaloupe Ido.

SOURCE: J. A. Demonchaux Co., 827 North Kansas, Topeka,
Kansas 66608.

COOKING TIP 1
Desserts served in the nouvelle cuisine manner are often sherbets
made of exotic fruits such as papaya, kiwi fruit, or passion fruit.
Cantaloupe serves as well. Consult a basic cookbook for a fresh
sherbet recipe and substitute cantaloupe for the fruit called for.
Keep in mind that recipes for sherbets made from fruit juice
rather than fruit pulp will not serve as a guide. Serve the sherbet
with slices or balls of cantaloupe which have been marinated in
a small quantity of Kirsch. This dessert is delightfully refreshing
and very low in calories.

Onions

*

Ah, the wonderful world of onions. If asparagus is the king of
vegetables, then surely onions are queen. Where would cooks be
without onions, since they are basic to all fine cuisine? But so
many different varieties are cultivated—where does one begin to
select? Which are sweet? Which are pungent? Which grow from
sets? Which from seeds? Well, here it is all sifted out for you.
Onions are divided into two categories: green onions and "keeping" onions. Green onions are dug from the garden as needed
through the growing season. "Keepers" are harvested for storage
through the winter.

Common onions—that is, the yellow variety found in all
markets—are "keeping" onions. They are strong in taste. Yellow
Ebenezer, Yellow Globe, and a vestige of the eighteenth century,
Wethersfield Red, are but a few varieties. Ebenezers and Globe
sets are commonly available in your garden centers. Wethersfield
Red is available from Comstock Ferre Seed Company, Wethersfield, Connecticut 16109.

Green onions—that is, those harvested during the season
and eaten fresh from the garden—include bottle, globe, bunch-
ing, and Egyptian walking onions. These are the onions that you
will want to grow. They generally do not keep well.

73

BOTTLE ONIONS

HARDINESS: Annual, very hardy.

WHEN TO PLANT: In early spring, as soon as ground is workable.

SPACING: In rows 1 foot apart, ultimately 3 inches apart.

DEPTH: About 1 inch deep.

HARVEST TIME: Throughout season as needed. Early onions are excellent as scallions; later onions are full grown.

Bottle onions are available in two colors, red and white. These are the varieties found braided and hanging in kitchens and restaurants in Europe. They resemble short, fat cucumbers and have the great advantage of slicing evenly, making them particularly useful for homemade relishes. They are not good "keepers," but are delicate and mild in taste and are especially attractive to gourmands. They are considered the aristocrats of the onion family.

HOW TO GROW BOTTLE ONIONS
As soon as soil is workable, in early spring, plant three seeds per inch, about 1 inch deep in rows 1 foot apart in full sun. Fertilize with 5-10-5 fertilizer or organic mixture and water thoroughly after planting. As the seedlings grow, thin to 3 inches apart to allow space for full-size onions. Thin to 1/2 to 1 inch apart for scallions or cocktail onions. These onions are generally fully mature in from 130 to 150 days.

GARDENER'S TIP 1
During the growing season, pick the flower-bearing stalks off at the base.

GARDENER'S TIP 2
You might want to try keeping these onions in braids. You may have luck and you may not, but do not expect them to remain edible until spring. To cure these onions, when you notice that the tops of the bulbs have that dry, transparent skin on them, gently pull them from the ground. Do not cut the green tops off the onions. Lay them on a screen in full sun for about a week and

let them dry out. When the stalk at the neck of the onion is completely dry, the onions are ready to air in a shaded area. Let them dry for several weeks and then prepare for storage. Cut the dry greens from the bulbs and store them in meshed onion bags. Or, if you prefer, leave the tops on and braid them. In either case, store the onions in a cool, dry place until ready to use.

PESTS: All onions are relatively pest-free.

VARIETY: Red Torpedo.

SOURCE: Gurney Seed, Yankton, South Dakota 57079.

VARIETY: A new import from Denmark called 153 O.W.A.

SOURCE: Epicure Seeds, Box 69, Avon, New York 14414.

GLOBE ONIONS

HARDINESS: Very hardy annual.

WHEN TO PLANT: In early spring, as soon as ground is workable.

SPACING: In rows 1 foot apart, ultimately 4 inches apart.

DEPTH: At soil line of seedlings, or just below soil line for sets.

HARVEST TIME: Throughout the season as needed. Early onions are scallion size, later full grown.

Globe onions are known in the markets as Bermuda onions. They are round, milder in taste than the common onion, and grow to impressive size in red, white, and yellow. They generally do not keep well. Bermudas are planted from seedlings or sets. Immature white Globe Bermuda Onions can be used as cocktail onions or in stew.

HOW TO GROW GLOBE ONIONS
As soon as soil is workable, plant sets or seedlings 2 inches apart, 1 inch deep, in rows 1 foot apart. All onions prefer full sun. Water thoroughly and keep well watered during the season. During the early part of the season, pull every other plant and use as scal-

lions. When the tops dry in the fall, dig the onions, use them, or slice or mince them in your food processor and freeze.

GARDENER'S TIP 1
Be sure to pick the flower-bearing stalks at the base during the growing season.

PESTS: All onions are relatively pest-free.

VARIETY: Southport Globe is one of the best.

SOURCE: W. J. Unwin Limited, Box 9, Farmingdale, New Jersey 07727.

COOKING TIP 1
During the fresh tomato season, I use onions in this way. Skin and slice 2 pounds of vine-ripened tomatoes and place them in a bowl. Grate 2 sweet onions and mix them with the tomatoes. Place the bowl in the freezer until the mixture just begins to form ice crystals. Remove it, add an oil and vinegar dressing, and serve immediately. During the hot summer months, this near-iced salad is very refreshing.

EGYPTIAN ONIONS (Walking Onions)

HARDINESS: Annual, very hardy.

WHEN TO PLANT: From early spring to late fall.

SPACING: In a bed, 6 inches apart in all directions.

DEPTH: Just below the soil's surface.

HARVEST TIME: Throughout the season as needed.

Egyptian or walking onions are small onion bulbs, which produce bulbils on top of the green stalks instead of flowers. When the top falls, the bulbils plant themselves. Plant them in full sun where they will remain undisturbed by annual Rototilling. The advantage of growing these onions is that they can be harvested very early in the spring. Keep in mind that when you dig them, leave several in the ground so that they can resow themselves.

HOW TO GROW EGYPTIAN ONIONS

Plant sets or bulbils in a section of the garden that will remain undisturbed. Set them about 6 inches apart, just below the soil line.

GARDENER'S TIP 1

These onions are virtually infallible. Plant them in beds rather than rows. Although not a gardener's primary source of onions, they come in very handy early in the season for flavoring sauces or soups before your other onions are ready to dig.

PESTS: Egyptian onions are pest-free.

VARIETY: Egyptian or Walking Onions.

SOURCE: Comstock Ferre Seed Company, Wethersfield, Connecticut 06109.

Paprika Peppers

HARDINESS: Annual, tender.

WHEN TO PLANT: Start seeds indoors 6 to 8 weeks before all danger of frost is past. Set outside mid-May to early June.

SPACING: Indoors: Sow 1 inch apart; outdoors: Plant seedlings 2 feet apart.

DEPTH: Indoors: 1/2 inch; outdoors: Just below the soil line of seedling.

HARVEST TIME: Pick in July when peppers are red and ripe.

Paprika is the Hungarian word for red pepper. And spanking-fresh paprika is difficult to obtain unless you happen to be fortunate enough to live near a purveyor who imports the spice from Hungary. But with no more effort than it takes to grow domestic peppers, you can grow the variety used to produce fresh paprika. Making your own is simply a matter of growing the vegetable properly, drying the fruits, and grinding them to powder consistency. The Hungarian Wax pepper, which has a long, slender, pointed pod about 4 or 5 inches long, will produce a mild and mellow-flavored spice with a rich, red color.

HOW TO GROW HUNGARIAN WAX PEPPERS

Start the seeds indoors in flats filled with a mixture of sand, peat moss, and vermiculite. Plan on sowing about 6 to 8 weeks before setting plants out in mid-May or early June. Sow about 1/2 inch deep, 1 inch apart, water thoroughly, and place in a warm area, about 70 or 80 degrees.

In approximately 1 week, when the seeds have germinated and small leaves appear, place the plants next to a sunny window (southern exposure preferred). Or place them under fluorescent lights for about 12 to 14 hours a day.

About 2 weeks before planting time, harden off the plants by placing them outdoors during the daylight hours.

After all danger of frost is past, plant your pepper plants about 2 feet apart in a sunny, well-drained, fertile spot. Peppers prefer light, friable soil, not too rich in nitrogen. Too much nitrogen forces the plants to go to leaf with sparse vegetable production. Transplant on a cloudy day in order to avoid wilting problems. Water thoroughly at planting time and throughout the summer.

Be advised that cutworms can be a problem with peppers. Simply fashion a collar of cardboard or other material at the base of the plant and sink it into the ground about 1 inch.

By July, the pepper plants will produce small, yellow-green fruits which will gradually turn brilliant red as they ripen. When ripe and red, pick them and prepare for drying.

GARDENER'S TIP 1

Peppers are almost pest-free; however, blossom-end rot may attack your plants. Apply nonhazardous doses of lime and superphosphate to counter a calcium deficiency. This problem is likely to occur after dry spells during the early part of the season. Conscientious watering will help you to avoid this problem.

VARIETY: Hungarian Wax Pepper.

SOURCES: Burpee Seed Company, Warminster, Pennsylvania 18991, or Clinton, Iowa 52732; George W. Park Seed Company, Greenwood, South Carolina 29647.

COOKING TIP 1

Use only the "walls" of the peppers. Discard the seeds, tissue, and stems. Place the "walls" on a screen in a warm, shady, dry place and let them dry out. Or dry them in a slow oven (150 degrees) until brittle. When the peppers are bone dry, grind them with a food processor or by hand with a mortar and pestle. Store in glass jars or other moistureproof containers in the refrigerator. For the freshest spice, save the brittle "walls" and grind the spice as needed.

COOKING TIP 2

Of course paprika is an essential ingredient in one of the world's great cuisines, that of Hungary. A delicious mushroom dish is easily prepared by sautéing 1 pound fresh mushrooms in 2 tablespoons butter and 1 teaspoon fresh lemon juice. After about 5 minutes, add 2 tablespoons minced onion, 1 teaspoon flour, 2 teaspoons paprika, 1/2 teaspoon salt, and a dash of cayenne pepper. Mix the ingredients and add 1/3 cup sour cream. Heat, but don't boil. Serve hot.

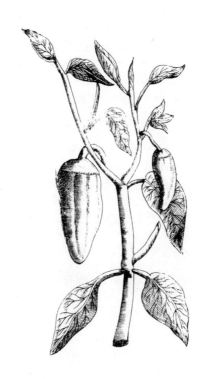

Petits Pois

PEAS

HARDINESS: Annual, very hardy.

WHEN TO PLANT: In early spring, as soon as ground is workable.

SPACING: Double rows about 1 foot apart. Allow a 2-foot separation between every three rows for better ventilation. Plant fifteen seeds per foot.

DEPTH: 1 inch.

HARVEST TIME: 6 to 7 weeks.

These are the tiny little beebee peas favored by the French. There is no trick to growing these vegetables. If you've grown domestic varieties, you can grow these, as cultivation is exactly the same. The secret is knowing when to harvest.

HOW TO GROW PETITS POIS

Peas are an early crop, suffering in the heat and drought of summer, so you must plant them early. Late March to early April is probably the best time. They like full sun and fairly rich soil in order to produce abundantly. Before you plant the seed, work in compost, rotted manure, and some 5-10-5 fertilizer or organic mixture. Then place 1 inch of unfortified soil on the bottom of a 3-inch-deep row. Plant the seeds fifteen per foot. Cover with 1 to 2 inches of soil and tamp down. The French petits pois grow about 16 inches high, so some support will be necessary for your plants. You can place 2-foot-high twigs in the soil along the row, or build a support with stakes and 3-foot-high chicken wire. After harvesting, simply pull up the stakes and roll up the wire and save it for the following year.

When your plants are about 6 to 8 inches high, sprinkle some 5-10-5 fertilizer or organic mixture lightly on either side of the rows. But make sure you do not overdo it, for peas, being legumes, extract nitrogen from the air. Take care not to allow the granules of fertilizer or organic mixture to come in contact with the leaves of the plant. Keep well cultivated to prevent weeds.

GARDENER'S TIP 1
The secret to delectable petits pois is to pick them when they are very young. I've found the best way to determine when they are ready is to pick one, open it up, and eat the sugar-sweet morsels. If they taste good that way, they'll taste even better on the table.

GARDENER'S TIP 2
Rabbits and birds feast on peas, so enclose your garden with fence. If birds prove to be a nuisance as the pods develop, net your pea patch.

GARDENER'S TIP 3
You do have the option of inoculating your peas before planting. Purchase legume inoculant from a garden center, moisten the seed, pour on the powder, roll the seed in the powder, coating it generously, and plant the seed. Your germination success and yield will be greater.

GARDENER'S TIP 4
After the vines have spent, do not pull them out, but cut them off at the base. The roots add nitrogen and other nutrients to the soil.

PESTS: Pea weevils are brown with gray, black, and white markings and are 1/5 inch long. They damage blossoms and lay egg clusters on young pods. To control use a 57 percent Malathion

EC solution (2 tablespoons to 1 gallon of water) and spray the plants while they blossom and before the first pods form. Stop spraying 7 days before harvest. Seed maggots sometimes burrow into seeds, damaging the emerging young plants. You can use Diazinon WP (1 tablespoon to 1 gallon of water) and drench the seed furrows before planting. Wood ashes mixed into the soil before planting are thought to also help to ward off these pests.

VARIETIES: The choice is limited, but both offerings are superb. Petit Provençal is early and very productive. A new variety, Fabina, is a gourmet treat as well. Both freeze well.

SOURCE: J. A. Demonchaux Co., Inc., 827 North Kansas, Topeka, Kansas 66609. As far as I know, this is the only source for these seeds.

COOKING TIP 1
Steam the peas for several minutes, serve with melted butter, and enjoy them. God forbid, don't make a cream sauce for them. As with most epicurean vegetables, they are at their best served plain with butter.

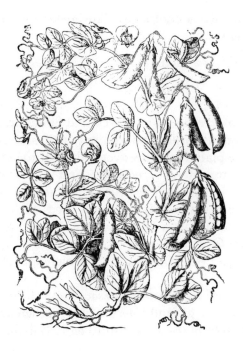

Radish

ORIENTAL DAIKON: (Winter Radish)

HARDINESS: Annual, very hardy.

WHEN TO PLANT: In early spring, as soon as ground is workable.

SPACING: In rows 1 foot apart. Sow seeds thinly and thin out to 4 inches apart.

DEPTH: About 1/2 inch.

HARVEST TIME: In fall.

For the most part, radishes in the United States are nothing more than red, wooden marbles, packed in plastic and used as garnish to add color to platters of other vegetables or to salads. In the Far East, radishes are eaten as frequently and with as much gusto as are potatoes in this country. And they are prepared in many different ways: steamed, boiled, stir-fried, pickled, and deep-fried. There are at least a dozen or so different kinds of radishes available from Oriental seed specialty houses. I suggest that you order several and experiment to find which appeal to your taste.

HOW TO GROW DAIKON RADISH
Plant as soon as the ground is workable and then again at 2-week intervals throughout the season until early fall. Place your bed in

full sun, and fortify the soil with a good sprinkling of 5-10-5 fertilizer or organic mixture. Sow the seeds thinly about 1/2 inch deep and when seedlings are about 1 inch high thin to 4 inches apart. (Keep in mind that daikon radishes come in many shapes and sizes, so be sure to check your seed package for thinning instructions.)

For small, young daikon, harvest in about 4 weeks. For fully mature specimens, harvest in about 2 months. Again, check package instructions for harvest time with individual varieties.

GARDENER'S TIP 1

If you have had trouble with root maggots tunneling through your domestic radishes, chances are you will have the same problem with Oriental varieties. Apply Diazinon crystals according to instructions on the package. Wood ashes worked into the soil may possibly help ward off these pests.

VARIETIES: There are many.

SOURCES: Kitazawa Seed Co., 356 W. Taylor St., San Jose, California 95110; Tsang and Ma International, P.O. Box 294, Belmont, California 94002.

COOKING TIP 1

Daikon is a very versatile vegetable. To prepare for cooking, peel and cut as you would carrots. The most obvious way to prepare them is to stir-fry or steam and serve with your favorite Oriental condiments. But the Japanese shred 1/2 pound daikon and 1/2 pound carrots, soak them in cold water for 30 minutes, drain, and then combine them with a salad dressing made of 1 cup vinegar, 1/2 cup sugar, 1 teaspoon salt, and 1/2 teaspoon monosodium glutamate. All ingredients are heated just until the sugar dissolves. Use only enough to moisten the shredded vegetables. The rest stores well in the refrigerator.

Radish

FRENCH BREAKFAST

⌀

HARDINESS: Annual, very hardy.

WHEN TO PLANT: In early spring, as soon as ground is workable. Successive plantings every 7 days until the heat of summer, and then again in the fall.

SPACING: Rows about 1 foot apart; plant seeds 1/2 inch apart and thin to 1 inch.

DEPTH: 3/4 inch.

HARVEST TIME: 18 days.

These are probably the mildest, sweetest radishes grown. As with all radishes, there's nothing to growing them. They're small, about half the size of an adult's pinky, and believe it or not, a treat even at breakfast time.

HOW TO GROW FRENCH BREAKFAST RADISHES
Plant as soon as the ground is workable and then again at 7-day intervals throughout the spring. The secret of producing mild and sweet radishes is quick growth, so accommodate them with the proper growing conditions: that is, full sun, a good dose of water at least once a week, and an initial fortification of the soil with sprinklings of 5-10-5 fertilizer or organic mixture. Sow the seeds

3/4 inch deep, about 1/2 inch apart, and thin to 1 inch when seedlings are about 1 inch high. Harvest in 18 days.

GARDENER'S TIP 1
If you find when you dig your radishes that they have split, they are too old. Dispose of them.

PESTS: Plant a trial run to see if root maggots tunnel into your crop. If so, when you plant your subsequent crops, apply Diazinon crystals as directed on the package. Wood ashes are sometimes thought to help alleviate this problem. Other than this pest, radishes are pest-free.

VARIETY: 18-Day Radish.

SOURCE: J. A. Demonchaux Co., Inc., 827 North Kansas, Topeka, Kansas 66609.

COOKING TIP 1
Try these just with sweet butter and a little salt and pepper. That is how the French eat them.

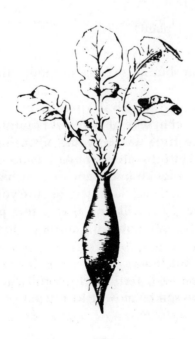

Rhubarb

HARDINESS: Perennial, hardy.

WHEN TO PLANT: In early spring, as soon as ground is workable.

SPACING: 3 to 4 feet apart.

DEPTH: Soil line of plant.

HARVEST TIME: 2 to 3 years after planting, in early to late spring in particular, but all seasons in moderation, if desired.

After initial planting, rhubarb is virtually maintenance-free, all the more reason to set in several plants. A bountiful supply of this delicious vegetable-fruit will be yours all spring long and well into the summer. Unfortunately, rhubarb is not adapted to most parts of the South, though in certain areas of higher elevation it does grow fairly well. Check locally to be sure your area is appropriate for growing. You will find that a few plants along the garden fence will supply you with all that a family can use.

HOW TO GROW RHUBARB

Any deep, well-drained, fertile soil in full sun is suitable for rhubarb. Spade the soil or plow it to a depth of 12 to 16 inches and mix in rotted manure, leaf mold, compost, or other form of organic matter. Since rhubarb is planted in hills 3 to 4 feet apart, it is generally sufficient to prepare each hill separately.

The best way to start your rhubarb is to purchase plants in the early spring. Most garden centers have a supply of this plant, but if not, you can order from almost any mail order nursery.

Set the plants out at soil level. You can easily see this by looking at the stem of your specimen. The plant you buy was grown in soil, so just set it at the same level. Each year, in either spring or fall, top-dress the planting with a heavy application of rotted manure, compost, or 10-6-4 commercial fertilizer. About 1 pound of this per hill will suffice.

At some point during the season, a large bulbous seed bud will develop at the tip of each plant. Remove these immediately, for if left to develop, they will divert valuable nutrients from the edible stalks.

Every seven or eight years the plants will become too thick and will produce only slender edible stems. Dig these in the fall, split the roots into sections having at least two to three buds as well as a heavy root system, and replant in a different section of the garden. Each division will develop into a new plant.

Do not pick any stems the first year. Pick sparingly the second year, and then as much as you like after that. To pick rhubarb, remove the stem by gripping it near the base and pulling and twisting to one side. The stalk will break easily from the plant. Do not pick any more than one-third of the stems during any given year.

GARDENER'S TIP 1
Remove all leaves from the stems after you have picked them. Do not under any circumstances use them for food, as they contain poisonous substances, including oxalic acid.

PESTS: There are none.

VARIETIES: Canada Red, Crimson, MacDonald, Red Valentine, and Victoria are all standard varieties.

SOURCES: Most garden centers and mail order houses.

COOKING TIP 1

Believe it or not, rhubarb can be made into a splendid and refreshing punch, either with or without alcohol. Consult *The Spice
Cookbook* by Avanelle Day and Lillie Stuckey for the nonalcohol
version. Rum and/or cognac can be added for a more potent
libation.

Romano Beans

HARDINESS: Annual, tender.

WHEN TO PLANT: In late spring, mid-May to early June, when all danger of frost is past. Like other beans, Romanos rot in damp, cool soil. Then plant again every 2 weeks for successive crops.

SPACING: Rows about 2 feet apart. Plant seeds about 2 to 3 inches apart.

DEPTH: 1 to 2 inches.

HARVEST TIME: 6 to 7 weeks.

These are the beans that northern Italians use in cooking. They are fleshier, with a more intense taste than our domestic varieties. Again, as with so many gourmet vegetables, there are no tricks to growing them. If you can grow domestic string beans, you can grow Romano beans.

HOW TO GROW ROMANO BEANS

Plant in full sun in moderately fertile soil. At planting time, work a little 5-10-5 fertilizer or organic mixture into each row before you sow the seeds. Use a hoe to make a row about 1 inch in depth and plant the seeds 2 to 3 inches apart. Cover with soil and tamp down. Throughout the growing season cultivate to keep free of weeds, and water well during droughts. About 50 days later, when the beans are about 4 1/2 inches in length, pick them. Cook them or freeze for use later.

GARDENER'S TIP 1
Protect against rabbits, who will make mincemeat out of seedlings when they emerge.

GARDENER'S TIP 2
Do not allow Romano beans to grow old, as they become tough and quite inedible.

GARDENER'S TIP 3
Cultivate beans only in the heat of the day.

GARDENER'S TIP 4
Romano beans are not hybridized, so at the end of the picking season, allow several plants to grow to maturity. Then, when the pods are dry, pick them, shell them, and use the seeds for next year's planting.

GARDENER'S TIP 5
All legumes benefit from inoculation before planting the seeds, at least the first few times. Purchase an inoculant from your local garden center, moisten the seeds, pour on the powder, roll the seed in the powder, and plant.

PESTS: Mexican bean beetles, which are oval and copper-colored, and bean leaf beetles, which are red to yellow with black spots, may attack your plants. Hand-pick or use a 5 percent rotenone WP (5 tablespoons to 1 gallon water).

VARIETY: Roma.

SOURCE: George W. Park Seed Co., Greenwood, South Carolina 29647.

COOKING TIP 1
The Romans prepare these as follows: For 3 pounds of beans, 2 tablespoons of minced onion are sautéed until translucent. Two tablespoons of olive oil are added to the skillet, followed by the beans, salt and pepper, and 1/3 cup water. Simmer until tender, about 6 to 7 minutes, drain, and serve immediately.

Shallots

HARDINESS: Annual, very hardy.

WHEN TO PLANT: In early spring, as soon as ground is workable.

SPACING: Rows 1 foot apart, plant sets 6 inches apart.

DEPTH: With pointed tops just below soil surface.

HARVEST TIME: Late August, early September.

America's culinary revolution of the past decade or so has created a demand for foods formerly relatively unknown in this country. One of these is the highly praised member of the onion family, the shallot (pronounced with the accent on the final syllable, incidentally). It resembles a small tulip bulb, with a shiny brown skin which when peeled reveals a purple outer surface. The taste of the shallot clove lies somewhere between an onion and garlic and is highly esteemed in classic French and northern Italian cuisine when a distinctive onion taste is desired.

HOW TO GROW SHALLOTS
Anyone who has grown onions can grow shallots. Culture and requirements are exactly the same. Order your shallot sets from a mail order seed house, or if they are available in your supermar-

ket or a specialty store, you can plant those. Shallots like a light, friable, well-drained soil with lots of humus or compost worked into it to ensure a constant source of nutrients for a heavy yield.

If your sets consist of an entire bulb like a garlic, which you might buy in the market, separate each bulb into individual cloves. Place them in the ground in full sun, about 4 inches apart with the blunt end down. Cover them with soil so that the pointed tops are just below the level of the garden soil. Once planted, water them well. In about 10 days or so, they will begin to grow.

During the season, keep the soil around your shallots well cultivated. Weed competition will dwarf your harvest at the end of the season. During drought, water thoroughly.

Wait until late August or early September to harvest. When the leaves have turned brown and have almost died down, dig the shallots and place them on a screen in the sun to dry. Provide adequate ventilation during the drying period. The following week, cut off the tops, rub the dead leaves, skin, and dry soil off, and store the bulbs in a cool, dry place. Each shallot bulb will produce a cluster of six or more cloves.

GARDENER'S TIP 1
Some people have success planting shallots in the fall, wintering them over, and harvesting them early in the summer. I have not tried this method, as the spring planting has always been quite successful for me.

GARDENER'S TIP 2
Be sure to save enough shallots from your fall crop for the following year's planting.

GARDENER'S TIP 3
Shallots are almost infallible to grow.

PESTS: Few, if any.

VARIETIES: These are standard and simply called Shallots.

SOURCES: W. Atlee Burpee Seed Company, Warminster, Pennsylvania 18991, or Clinton, Iowa 52732; Gurney Seed and Nursery Co., Yankton, South Dakota 57079.

COOKING TIP 1

Check your cookbooks for recipes calling for shallots. For convenience, shallots can be chopped or minced in the food processer, frozen as is, and then used as needed. This will save you time mincing or chopping each time they are called for in a recipe.

COOKING TIP 2

If you find winter supermarket onions are too strong for some of your creations, simply substitute shallots for a milder taste. A superb salad dressing can be made with essence of shallot. To make the essence, boil 1 cup white wine. Add 4 tablespoons chopped shallots and boil for 5 minutes. Strain and combine with olive or walnut oil for a dressing your garden-grown greens deserve.

Snow Peas

HARDINESS: Annual, very hardy.

WHEN TO PLANT: In early spring, as soon as ground is workable.

SPACING: In rows about 2 feet apart. Plant seeds 3 inches apart.

DEPTH: 1 to 2 inches.

HARVEST TIME: 6 to 7 weeks.

These are the edible pea pods ubiquitous in Chinese cuisine. They can be mixed with other ingredients in the preparation of classic dishes or can be stir-fried and eaten alone. Snow peas are rarely available fresh in the markets, and the frozen product is not only expensive but a pale comparison to these sweet fresh morsels.

HOW TO GROW SNOW PEAS

Like petits pois, snow peas are an early crop, averse to the heat and dry spells of summer, so plant as soon as the ground is workable. Full sun and rich soil will produce the best crop, so fortify the soil with compost, rotted manure, and 5-10-5 fertilizer or organic mixture. Plant the seeds about 3 inches apart and cover with 1 to 2 inches of soil. Tamp down and water thoroughly.

Snow peas can grow to a height of 6 to 7 feet if conditions

are right, so be sure to provide support. I have found the easiest solution to supporting the vines is to tack plastic netting against posts which I have hammered into the ground. A minimum height of 5 feet is recommended.

As the plants grows, keep them well watered and cultivate to prevent weed growth. When the plants are about 1 foot high, sprinkle 5-10-5 fertilizer or organic mixture on either side of them.

GARDENER'S TIP 1

After 6 weeks, sample some of your snow peas. They should be flat, about 3 to 4 inches long, and they should taste as sweet as sugar. Do not let them grow too large or "fill out," as the pods will be tough and stringy in texture and quite bitter. If they do, shell and use like ordinary peas.

GARDENER'S TIP 2

As with other peas, take precautions against rabbits, as they will devour your young plants. Fence is recommended. Birds may also be a problem when the young pods develop. Plastic netting should solve this problem.

GARDENER'S TIP 3

Inoculating the seeds before planting will ensure good plant growth and high yield in new planting areas. Purchase some inoculant at your garden center, moisten the seeds, pour on the powder, roll the seeds in it, and plant.

GARDENER'S TIP 4

As with petits pois and other peas, do not pull the vines out by the roots when they have spent, but cut them off at the base. The nodules of nitrogen contained will fortify the soil.

GARDENER'S TIP 5

At the end of the bearing season, around the end of June, permit a portion of your crop to "fill out." Do not eat them, but dry them to use the following year when you plant your crop.

PESTS: Pea weevils are brown with gray, black, and white markings and are 1/5 inch long. They damage blossoms and lay egg clusters on young pods. Use a 57 percent Malathion EC solution (2 tablespoons to 1 gallon of water) and spray the plants while they blossom and before the first pods form. Stop spraying 7 days before harvest. Seed maggots sometimes burrow into seeds, damaging the emerging young plants. If you have this problem, take precautions the following year. Use Diazinon WP (1 tablespoon to 1 gallon water) and drench the seed furrows before planting.

VARIETY: Snow Peas.

SOURCES: Kitazawa Seed Co., 356 W. Taylor Street, San Jose, California 95110; Tsang and Ma International, P.O. Box 294, Belmont, California 94002.

COOKING TIP 1
Pick your snow peas just before you are ready to cook them. Many classic Chinese dishes include snow peas. Seafood kow, fu yung chicken, and the superb filet mignon kow are examples. See Irene Kuo's *The Key to Chinese Cooking* for a recipe using snow peas.

Spaghetti Squash

HARDINESS: Annual, tender.

WHEN TO PLANT: After all danger of frost, from mid-May to early June.

SPACING: In hills 4 to 6 feet apart, two to four plants per hill.

DEPTH: 1/2 inch.

HARVEST TIME: About 90 to 100 days.

Spaghetti squash is another of the recent additions to the gourmet vegetable scene in the United States. It has only been in the last year or so that seeds for this vegetable have been available in seed racks at your local garden center. Cultivation is the same as for other summer squash such as zucchini and yellow squash. When this vegetable is cooked, the flesh separates into spaghettilike strands with a slightly crunchy texture. It is, to say the least, very good to eat and, if you are weight-conscious, very low in calories.

HOW TO GROW SPAGHETTI SQUASH
Plant your spaghetti squash in full sun after all danger of frost is over. Like cucumbers and melons, squash is planted in small mounds measuring about 1 1/2 feet across, set 4 feet apart. Dig

about a shovelful of rotted manure and compost into the hollow of your squash mound. Also mix in about 1 pound of 5-10-5 fertilizer or 2 pounds of organic mixture. Then cover the nutrients with soil. Plant three to five seeds in a circle near the center of the mound and cover with 1/2 inch of soil. After the seeds have germinated, remove all but two or three plants per hill. If you have fertilized at planting time, additional amounts of fertilizer will not be necessary during the growing season. Keep well watered during dry periods and remove weed growth as it appears.

GARDENER'S TIP 1
Spaghetti squash should be picked when young and tender. Your crop should be ready in about 90 to 100 days. If your fingernail cannot puncture the skin, the squash is too old, so be sure to harvest when the fruits are young. If you permit the squash to remain on the vine until it becomes large and pulpy, the results will be disappointing and your plant will probably not bear much more produce.

GARDENER'S TIP 2
To conserve moisture, keep weeds down, and to ensure warm soil for rapid growth, black plastic laid down on your squash patch will do wonders. After you've prepared your bed, cover the entire area with the synthetic mulch. Then cut holes where you wish to plant the seeds and put them in place.

GARDENER'S TIP 3
I have not had difficulties with rabbits eating spaghetti squash, so I do not cover my crop with chicken wire.

GARDENER'S TIP 4
Spaghetti squash will store well in a cool, dry place.

PESTS: Spaghetti squash seems to be relatively pest-free.

VARIETY: Simply Spaghetti Squash.

SOURCE: Seed racks at your local garden center.

COOKING TIP 1

Spaghetti squash can be prepared as you would any summer squash such as zucchini. At the Four Seasons Restaurant in New York City, they serve zucchini with pesto. Try spaghetti squash, using Marcella Hazan's pesto recipe in *The Classic Italian Cook Book.*

Sprouts

MUNG BEAN, ALFALFA
AND MIXED SALAD

This is an indoor crop easily grown. The bean sprouts you buy in a can in the Chinese food department of your supermarket, and other sprouts as well, can be germinated in your own kitchen in about 1 week. Just follow these instructions.

HOW TO GROW SPROUTS
1. Place the quantity of seeds required into a jar.
2. Secure the cap firmly and fill the jar three-fourths full with warm water.
3. Shake the jar vigorously for about 10 to 15 seconds.
4. Drain the water away without totally removing the lid.
5. Repeat steps two, three, and four two times a day until the sprouts are ready to eat (about a week or so).

Bean sprouts are basic to Chinese cooking. They also make delicious and very nutritious additions to salads throughout the year. Mung beans are what the Chinese use to produce bean sprouts, but alfalfa and a rather enticing collection of other seeds for sprouting are available from several sources. The best source is listed below.

VARIETIES: Alfalfa, mung beans, fenugreek, and mixed salad seeds.

SOURCE: Thompson and Morgan, Inc., P.O. Box 100, Farming-dale, New Jersey 07727.

COOKING TIP 1
Alfalfa sprouts are delightful in little finger sandwiches. Simply spread soft butter on thin white bread and fill with sprouts. Fenugreek sprouts have a delicious spicy flavor with a touch of maple.

COOKING TIP 2
The Chinese stir-fry whole mung bean sprouts for about 1 minute and add a few drops of sesame oil and vinegar.

Sugar Snap Peas

HARDINESS: Annual, very hardy.

WHEN TO PLANT: In early spring, as soon as ground is workable.

SPACING: Rows 2 1/2 feet to 3 feet apart. Plant seeds 1 to 2 inches apart.

DEPTH: 1 to 2 inches.

HARVEST TIME: About 10 weeks.

Truly a triumph, these superb peas were developed in this country and introduced only within the past four years. I have seen them for sale in Manhattan's most elegant food emporiums for as much as seven dollars a pint. Ridiculous! If you've grown regular peas, you can grow these. Cultivation and yield are the same. And do believe the glowing reports you read in the seed catalogs about these vegetables. They are everything they say and more. They are a cross between the Oriental snow pea and the conventional pea, with sugar sweet pods and full firm peas inside. You don't shell them, but simply cut them up, pod and all, and cook the entire vegetable or eat them raw in salads.

HOW TO GROW SUGAR SNAP PEAS

Plant as early as soil is workable. As with other peas, full sun and reasonable soil will produce a bumper crop. Fortify the soil with compost, rotted manure, and some 5-10-5 fertilizer or organic mixture. Sow seeds 1 to 2 inches apart in rows 2 1/2 to 3 feet apart. Cover with 1 to 2 inches of fine soil. Tamp down and keep moist. The seeds should germinate in 7 to 10 days.

Sugar peas are vigorous growers and can attain a height of 6 feet, so you must provide support. See snow pea cultivation for plastic netting and stake technique.

GARDENER'S TIP 1

Be sure to pick these vegetables when they are young. The pod should be filled out but still tender. The taste test is the best way to ascertain whether or not they are ready to eat.

GARDENER'S TIP 2

As with other peas, rabbits and birds may present problems. Fence your crop to ward off rabbits and net the peas to deter the birds.

GARDENER'S TIP 3

As with other peas, do not pull vines out when spent. Cut off at base and let the roots add nitrogen to the soil.

GARDENER'S TIP 4

Inoculate your seeds before planting to ensure good plant growth and high yield in new planting areas. Purchase inoculant at your local garden center, moisten the seeds, pour on the powder, roll the seed in the powder, and plant.

PESTS: Pea weevils are brown with gray, black, and white markings and are 1/5 inch long. They damage blossoms and lay egg clusters on young pods. Use a 57 percent Malathion EC solution (2 tablespoons to 1 gallon of water) and spray the plants while they blossom and before the first pods form. Stop spraying 7 days before harvest. Seed maggots sometimes burrow into seeds, damaging the emerging young plants. Use Diazinon WP (1 tablespoon to 1 gallon of water) and drench the seed furrows before planting.

VARIETIES: Sugar Snap Peas. This year George W. Park Seed Co., Inc., Greenwood, South Carolina 29647, introduced Pea Sugar Bon, a new variety which produces pods in just 56 days, about 2 weeks earlier than Sugar Snap. In addition, unlike its predecessor, whose vines grow to from 6 to 12 feet, the new variety produces manageable vines only 18 to 30 inches tall.

SOURCE: Seed racks at your local garden center.

COOKING TIP 1
Steam this vegetable and serve it with butter or stir-fry. You can also serve it cold and raw in a salad or with a dip.

Tabasco Peppers

HARDINESS: Annual, tender.

WHEN TO PLANT: Start seeds indoors 6 to 8 weeks before all danger of frost is over. Set outside mid-May to early June.

SPACING: Indoors: Sow seeds 1 inch apart; outdoors: Plant seedlings 2 feet apart.

DEPTH: Indoors: 1/2 inch; outdoors: About 1/2 inch deeper than soil line of seedlings.

HARVEST TIME: In July or August when peppers are red and ripe.

If you decide to grow these peppers, not only can you use them in cooking, but you can make your own tabasco sauce out of them. They are extremely hot in taste.

HOW TO GROW TABASCO PEPPERS
Start seed indoors in flats filled with a mixture of sand, peat moss, and vermiculite. Sow about 6 to 8 weeks before setting out in mid-May or early June when danger of frost is over. Plant about 1/2 inch deep, 1 inch apart, water the planting medium thoroughly, and place flats in a warm place, about 70 to 80 degrees.

About a week later the seeds will have germinated. Place the flat in a sunny window, southern exposure preferred. If you have Gro-Lux or fluorescent lights, place the plants under them for about 12 to 14 hours a day.

About a week before outdoor planting time, begin to harden your plants off. Place them outside in the sunshine for a few days and bring them in at night. After they have spent several days outdoors you can leave them out overnight as long as the nights are not cold.

When all danger of frost is over, or in early June when the seedlings are big enough to handle, plant them 2 feet apart in a sunny, well-drained, fertile spot. All peppers like friable, light soil with not too much nitrogen content. If there is an excess of this element, the plants will go to leaf with little vegetable production. Transplant your seedlings on a cloudy day if possible to avoid the sun's strong rays. Water thoroughly when planting and then throughout the summer.

Be sure to fashion collars for these plants, as cutworms may attack them. Simply encircle the plant with aluminum foil which you have sunk into the soil to a depth of about 1 inch.

By August, the pepper plants will produce small fruits which will turn brilliant red. When they are red and ripe, pick them and either use them for cooking or make tabasco sauce out of them.

GARDENER'S TIP 1
Tabasco pepper plants are attractive and can be worked into your flower bed or border.

PESTS: Regular watering during dry spells will help counter blossom-end rot.

VARIETY: Tabasco.

SOURCE: Nichols Garden Nursery, 1190 North Pacific Highway, Albany, Oregon 97321.

COOKING TIP 1
Here's how you can make your own tabasco sauce. Pick and wash peppers. Cut into pieces and discard stems, seeds, and white pithy interior. To make about 1 pint of tabasco sauce, you will need about 2 quarts of pepper "walls."

Place peppers in 2-quart pot. Add about 3/4 pint of white vinegar. Place 4 cloves minced garlic in pot. Cover with lid. Simmer slowly for about 1 1/2 hours. Taste to see if your tabasco sauce is hot enough. If it isn't, steep for 1/2 hour. Add additional vinegar if necessary. Strain, put in jar, and store in a cool, dry place. You can use your tabasco sauce immediately. It will keep indefinitely.

Tokyo Turnips

CHUNG CHOY

HARDINESS: Annual, hardy.

WHEN TO PLANT: In early spring, as soon as ground is workable.

SPACING: In rows 1 foot apart, plant seeds 1 inch apart, thinning to 4 inches apart.

DEPTH: 1/2 inch.

HARVEST TIME: In about 30 to 40 days for tender young specimens.

In the Far East, this vegetable is pickled, but I serve it raw in salads or with dips. Tokyo turnips are sweet, tender, pure white, very appetizing, and add a nutty crunchy texture to the crudités tray. They're very easily grown and a delight to the palate.

HOW TO GROW TOKYO TURNIPS

In early spring as soon as ground is workable, plant in full sun. Fertilize soil modestly with rotted manure, compost, and a sprinkling of 5-10-5 fertilizer or organic mixture. Keep well watered, cultivate to discourage weeds, and check for harvest in about 30 to 40 days. Pull when young, about 1 1/2 inches in diameter.

GARDENER'S TIP 1

Plant successive crops every 2 weeks until hot weather for a continuous supply, then plant again in the fall for a later crop.

PESTS: Tokyo turnips seem to be pest-free.

VARIETIES: Chung Choy, Tokyo Turnip, Tokyo Cross Hybrid Turnip.

SOURCES: Kitazawa Seed Co., 356 W. Taylor St., San Jose, California 95110; Tsang and Ma International, P.O. Box 294, Belmont, California 94002.

COOKING TIP 1

Tokyo turnips combine particularly well with snow peas when stir-fried. They can also be eaten raw with a dip or sliced in salad. The taste is peppery, akin to a very mild horseradish taste. The Orientals are particularly fond of pickled turnips along with other pickled vegetables. Consult Irene Kuo's *The Key to Chinese Cooking* for an authentic recipe.

Cherry Tomatoes

✑

HARDINESS: Annual, tender.

WHEN TO PLANT: Start seeds indoors 6 to 8 weeks before all danger of frost is past. Set outside mid-May to early June.

SPACING: Indoors: Sow 1 inch apart; outdoors: Plant seedlings about 1 foot apart.

DEPTH: Indoors: 1/2 inch; outdoors: Plant just below first pair of leaves on plant, regardless of soil line.

HARVEST TIME: 55 to 75 days.

During the height of the summer season, there is nothing quite like the taste of a massive beefsteak tomato or the spectacular new hybrid varieties of standard tomatoes. But for salads and hors d'oeuvre, these tiny versions make for tidy eating. You can just pick them and put them in your mouth, all in one bite. They are excellent salad and snack material for people on diets. No epicurean garden should be without at least several of these midget tomato plants.

HOW TO GROW CHERRY TOMATOES
Start your plants indoors from 6 to 8 weeks before outdoor planting time, mid-May to early June. Fill flats with a mixture of peat

moss, sand, and vermiculite. Plant seeds about 1/2 inch deep and 1 inch apart, water the planting medium thoroughly, and place the flat in a warm place, about 70 to 80 degrees.

When the seeds have germinated, in about a week, place the flat in a window that receives full southern sun. If you use Gro-Lux or other fluorescent lights, place the plants under them for about 12 to 14 hours a day.

About a week before planting time, harden your plants off. Place them outside during the day and bring them indoors at night. Then several days before planting, leave them out overnight *if* the nights are not too cold. By the end of that week leave them out overnight. When you transplant, if possible pick an overcast day. Hot sun might wilt your plants. Set the plants out in the garden about 1 foot to 18 inches apart.

As with other tomatoes, peppers, and eggplants, fashion a collar out of tin foil, cardboard or cut-off milk cartons to place around the stem. This will serve to ward off cutworms.

Before you plant, fertilize the ground sparingly with compost, rotted manure, and a sparse handful of 5-10-5 fertilizer or organic mixture. Set your plants in the soil with the lowest pair of leaves at soil level. Set the collar around each plant about 1 inch into the soil and about 3 inches above the soil line.

Stake the plants when they have grown to about 6 inches in height. Drive a 3-foot stake into the ground about 3 inches from the main stem of the plant. As your cherry tomatoes grow, tie them firmly to the stake.

Keep your plants weed-free and irrigate profusely during dry spells. All tomatoes require plenty of moisture in order to produce abundantly.

Harvest tomatoes as they turn a deep red color.

GARDENER'S TIP 1
Pinch all suckers that grow from between the leaf stems and the stalk. Let the plant energy form tomatoes instead of leaves.

GARDENER'S TIP 2
Cherry tomatoes adapt nicely to tub planting as well as indoor gardening. For a winter crop, sow seeds outdoors in August in pots. When they attain a height of about 6 inches, bring them

indoors to a sunny window. The plants should provide lots of cherry tomatoes throughout the winter.

GARDENER'S TIP 3
If you start these indoors well before planting time, you should have bearing plants by the time you are ready to set them out. In this way, you can have that fresh, vine-ripened-tasting tomato long before the standard tomatoes begin to bear.

PESTS: Tomato hornworm is green with diagonal lines on sides and a prominent spike or horn on the rear. Hand-pick the worms and immerse in kerosene or bleach. If you choose to spray, a 50 percent Sevin WP (2 tablespoons to 1 gallon of water) should be applied when the worms appear. A 5 percent rotenone WP (5 tablespoons to 1 gallon of water) will keep flea beetles under control. These are pinhead-sized, black, brown, or striped jumping beetles about 1/16 inch long.

VARIETIES: There are many. Tiny Tim is the earliest, Cherry Tomato the most popular.

SOURCES: Most mail order seed houses and racks at your garden center.

COOKING TIP 1
These tiny tomatoes make perfect hors d'oeuvre, as they are bite-size and can be picked up with the fingers. If you grow them in pots indoors in the winter, you won't have to resort to the tasteless variety available in the markets.

Roma Tomatoes

☙

HARDINESS: Annual, tender.

WHEN TO PLANT: Start seeds indoors 6 to 8 weeks before all danger of frost is past. Set outside from mid-May on.

SPACING: Indoors: Sow 1 inch apart; outdoors: Plant seedlings 2 feet apart.

DEPTH: Indoors: 1/2 inch; Outdoors: Plant just below first pair of leaves on plant, regardless of soil line.

HARVEST TIME: 72 to 76 days.

Sometimes you can find six-packs of this variety of tomato in your local garden center at planting time. To be sure you have planting stock, start seeds 6 to 8 weeks before setting-out time. These tomatoes are the paste-type or plum tomatoes from which Italian sauce is made. Cultivation is exactly the same as for standard tomatoes.

HOW TO GROW ROMA TOMATOES

Start seeds indoors from 6 to 8 weeks before outdoor planting time after danger of frost is past. Plant in flats filled with a mixture of soil, sand, peat moss, and vermiculite. Plant seeds about 1/2 inch deep, 1 inch apart, water the planting medium thoroughly, and place the flat in a warm place, about 70 to 80 degrees. After 1 week, when the seeds have germinated, place the flat in a sunny window, southern exposure preferred. If you have Gro-Lux or fluorescent lights, place plants under them for about 12 to 14 hours a day.

One week before outdoor planting time, begin to harden off your plants, that is, prepare them for the rigors of outdoor weather. Place them outside in a sunny spot for a few days, and bring them in at night. Then, let them remain outside on warm nights as well. If a cold snap is forecast, bring them inside for protection. By the end of 1 week, you can leave them out overnight. On an overcast day, set them in the garden.

Be sure to fashion collars out of tin foil or cardboard to wrap around the stem of each plant as you set it in the ground. This precaution will save you from the disaster of a cutworm invasion.

Fertilize the ground sparingly with compost, rotted manure, and a handful of 5-10-5 fertilizer or organic mixture. Do not overfertilize, as too much nitrogen in the soil will cause the plants to go to leaf. Set plants in the soil with the lower leaves at plant level. Notice that this is deeper than the soil level of the indoor planting medium.

When the plants have grown about 1 foot high, drive a 5-foot stake into the ground about 4 inches from the main stem of the plant. As the tomato plants grow, tie them firmly to the stake.

Be sure to keep your bed free from weeds and provide plenty of moisture during drought, at least 1 1/2 inches of water per week.

Harvest tomatoes when brilliant red in color.

PESTS: Tomato hornworms are green with diagonal lines on their sides and a prominent spike or horn on the rear. Hand-pick the worms and immerse in kerosene or bleach. If you choose to spray, a 50 percent Sevin WP (2 tablespoons to 1 gallon of water) should be applied as soon as these creatures appear. A 5 percent rotenone WP (5 tablespoons to 1 gallon of water) will keep flea beetles under control. These are pinhead size, black, brown, or striped, jumping beetles about 1/16 inch long.

VARIETIES: Roma, San Marzano.

SOURCES: W. Atlee Burpee Co., Warminster, Pennsylvania 18974, or Clinton, Iowa 52732; George W. Park Seed Co., Greenwood, South Carolina 29647.

COOKING TIP 1
Check Marcella Hazan's *The Classic Italian Cook Book* for a tomato sauce recipe. Use these tomatoes. And, television commercials notwithstanding, the bottled variety is a far cry from homemade.

Sorrel

SCHAV OR SOURGRASS

HARDINESS: Perennial, very hardy.

WHEN TO PLANT: In early spring, as soon as ground is workable.

SPACING: In rows 1 foot apart, sow thinly and thin to 1 foot apart.

DEPTH: 1/2 inch.

HARVEST TIME: 8 weeks after planting first year, then throughout the season in subsequent years.

This is the delightful tart green leaf which the French use to make *potage germiny*. Middle and Eastern European Christians and Jews have known sorrel well for centuries as sourgrass soup and Schav. Problem is when you encounter a recipe which says, "First take one pound of fresh sorrel . . . etc.," where on earth do you go to buy it? Growing your own is so simple there's no need to deprive yourself of this very special treat.

HOW TO GROW SORREL
Select a site in your garden that will remain undisturbed. Sorrel is perennial, so you will want to plant out of the way of the

annual Rototilling. If possible plant in a semishaded spot, as full sunlight tends to toughen the leaves somewhat.

Sorrel likes a rich loam, so fortify your soil with compost, rotted manure, bonemeal, and some 5-10-5 fertilizer or organic mixture. Dig in to a depth of about 1 foot. Each fall renew the soil with a top dressing of nutrients or fertilizer.

Sow seeds 1/2 inch deep in rows 1 foot apart. When the seedlings are about 1 inch high, thin them out to 6 inches apart. Then in the fall, when they have reached maturity, thin them to 1 foot apart.

GARDENER'S TIP 1
During the summer, flowering shoots will grow from the plant. As soon as they appear, cut them off, as they rob the plants of nourishment and prevent leaves from reaching maximum size.

GARDENER'S TIP 2
After your sorrel patch is established, pick leaves from the outside of the clump. This will permit the plant to spread vigorously.

GARDENER'S TIP 3
Rabbits relish sorrel, so provide fence to ward them off.

PESTS: There are few if any.

VARIETY: French Sorrel.

SOURCES: Nichols Garden Nursery, 1190 North Pacific Highway, Albany, Oregon 97321; Thompson and Morgan, Inc., Box 100, Farmingdale, New Jersey 07727; J. A. Demonchaux Co., 225 Jackson, Topeka, Kansas 66603.

COOKING TIP 1
The delectable *potage germiny* or sorrel soup served at the Ritz Hotel in Paris for generations is perhaps my favorite soup of all. Consult the *Escoffier Cook Book* for the recipe—the great chef himself created this delicacy.

Herbs and
Spices

Undoubtedly you don't have to be told about the difference in taste between fresh home-dried herbs and spices and those bought in the grocery store. Furthermore, you know the difference their use makes in the final taste of foods you prepare. Growing herbs and spices is, for the most part, a simple matter. Since many are disease- and pest-free, and in fact, will help protect vegetables, fruits, and berries from pests if planted close by, their cultivation makes good common sense.

Once you've started your collection, you'll undoubtedly want to add to it. Keep that in mind when planting, and allow space for the expansion of your herb garden.

Anise Seed

HARDINESS: Perennial, hardy.

WHEN TO PLANT: After all danger of frost, from mid-May to early June.

SPACING: Sow thinly and thin to 6 inches apart when seedlings are 2 inches high.

DEPTH: 1/4 inch.

HARVEST TIME: Mid to late summer, when flower heads dry.

Perennial anise has a flavored seed that is easily grown. It goes back to Virgil's time, when it was used in a spice cake eaten at the end of a meal in order to prevent indigestion. It was also served at the end of a marriage feast and is probably the origin of today's spicy wedding cake.

HOW TO GROW ANISE SEED

Sow seeds thinly, about 1/4 inch deep, in full sun after all danger of frost. Thin to 6 inches apart and keep weeded and watered during the summer. Anise does best in soil that is not too rich, so don't add fertilizer to your bed. In mid to late summer, white or rose-pink flowers will appear. When the flower heads dry, pick them and rub out the seeds. Store them in airtight containers in a cool, dry place.

GARDENER'S TIP 1
Anise seed can be saved through the winter and planted the following spring.

PESTS: Anise is pest-free.

VARIETY: Simply anise.

SOURCE: Nichols Garden Nursery, 1190 North Pacific Highway, Albany, Oregon 97321.

COOKING TIP 1
Anise seeds are traditionally used to add a licorice flavor to breads, cakes, cookies, and desserts. However, for a change of pace, when you prepare a compote of fresh or stewed fruits, simply put a few anise seeds into the sugar syrup when you cook it. It imparts a delicate taste to the fruit.

Basil

BASILICONE

HARDINESS: Annual, tender.

WHEN TO PLANT: After all danger of frost, from mid-May to early June.

SPACING: In rows 2 feet apart, sow seeds about 1/2 inch apart, ultimately thinning to 8 inches apart.

DEPTH: 1/4 inch.

HARVEST TIME: Early in the season to thin your bed and then until frost.

Basil has been called the "herb of kings," for it has been used in food cooked for royal personages since classical times. Undoubtedly you are familiar with it and probably have some on your spice shelf. Fresh basil is far superior to the dried variety for potent oils are lost in drying. Cultivation is simple. As you are undoubtedly aware, basil is basic to Italian cuisine.

HOW TO GROW BASIL

Plant basil when you plant your tomatoes, in mid-May to early June. And, in fact, if you plant some right next to your tomatoes, basil serves as a trap plant for pests which might infest them. Basil grows in full sun or semishade and needs only moderately fertile soil. Mix a little rotted manure, compost, or 5-10-5 fertilizer or organic mixture into your bed. Plant the seeds about 1/2 inch apart, 1/4 inch deep, in rows about 2 feet apart. After the seedlings emerge, thin to 8 inches apart. Use the seedlings in cooking. Then, pick leaves as you need them throughout the season.

GARDENER'S TIP 1
After the second set of leaves appear on your plant, pinch back the tips to increase bushiness.

GARDENER'S TIP 2
When the blossoms on your plants have just begun to open, take cuttings during the early morning for drying and winter storage. Rinse the leaves under cool water to remove the dirt and any insects that might be present and discard the damaged leaves. Then tie them with string and hang them upside down in the kitchen or any cool, dry place. Or spread them out on a screen or on cheesecloth in a dark, well-ventilated place away from direct sunlight to dry. Once dried, remove the leaves from the stems and store in airtight bottles in a cool, dark place for winter use.

GARDENER'S TIP 3
Be sure to let some of your crop go to seed. Collect the seed, store in a cool, dry place, and plant the following spring.

PESTS: Basil will ward off pests which attack other vegetables.

VARIETIES: There are two: Sweet Basil and Dark Opal. The foliage on the second variety is purplish in color rather than the bright green of the first.

SOURCE: Most garden centers or mail order houses.

COOKING TIP 1
Sweet basil leaves are used in vinegars, stews, fish, salads, tomato dishes, spaghetti, vegetable juices, and butter sauces. Tea made from the leaves is calming to the nerves.

COOKING TIP 2

Perhaps the most delicious way to enjoy basil is in Italian pesto. In Genoa, where this delicious sauce originated, they insist that it can be made only with a marble mortar. However, a delicious version can also be made either in a blender or food processor as well. You'll need 2 whole cups of basil leaves to make this wonderful concoction. You can serve it on fettucine, with potato gnocchi, or mixed into a hot or cold minestrone.

Caraway Seed

⊘

HARDINESS: Biennial, hardy.

WHEN TO PLANT: After all danger of frost, from mid-May to early June.

SPACING: Sow thinly and thin to 6 inches apart when seedlings are 1 inch high.

DEPTH: 1/4 inch.

HARVEST TIME: Since caraway is biennial, plant one year and harvest the seeds the following year.

Caraway seed is particularly prized for flavoring breads and rolls. Native to Northern Europe, it is also used in adding flavor to liqueurs. It is easily grown in the United States.

HOW TO GROW CARAWAY SEED
Sow seeds in full sun, about 1/4 inch deep. When plants are about 1 inch high, thin them to 6 inches apart. Nurture plants during the season, watering them regularly, and keep your patch weed-free. The following spring a sturdy stand of caraway will grow. By July or August, the plants will grow to a height of about 2 feet. White flowers in umbrels will adorn them. Eventually these will go to seed and your caraway seed crop will be ready

to harvest. Collect the seed, place in airtight containers, and store in a cool, dark, dry place.

GARDENER'S TIP 1
Be advised that caraway has a tendency to take over a garden, so you must be ruthless in restricting your crop to its allocated patch. Simply dig out or plow under any unwanted plants.

GARDENER'S TIP 2
Once you've collected your harvest, be sure to save enough seed for the following 2 years. Plant each year, for the following year's crop.

PESTS: Few, if any.

VARIETY: Caraway. There is only one variety.

SOURCE: Nichols Garden Nursery, 1190 North Pacific Highway, Albany, Oregon 97321.

COOKING TIP 1
In Belgium, caraway seed is added to the cooking water when Brussels sprouts are prepared. The taste complements the vegetables perfectly. Since caraway is a member of the carrot family, the slender taproot is very tasty and edible. You can also chop the leaves and add these to salads or soups. An exceptional hors d' oeuvre spread can be made by combining 1/3 cup crumbled blue cheese, 1/3 cup mayonnaise, 3 ounces cream cheese, 2 teaspoons caraway seed, and 1/4 teaspoon freshly ground pepper.

Catnip

HARDINESS: Perennial, hardy.

WHEN TO PLANT: From early spring through midsummer.

SPACING: Sow thinly in rows about 1 foot apart.

DEPTH: 1/4 inch.

HARVEST TIME: All through the season.

Well, after all, we can't forget old Puss, now can we? No need to tell you that catnip is a wonderful treat for your feline friends. It's easily grown and virtually indestructible. And some dogs, like my beagle, enjoy it as well.

HOW TO GROW CATNIP

From early spring to midsummer, purchase plants from your local garden center or through a mail order nursery. If you opt for plants, just set them in the ground, water them, and keep them weed-free. You can also grow catnip from seed. Plant thinly in rows about 1 foot apart, 1/4 inch deep. Catnip will thrive in full sun or partial shade and is not the slightest fussy about soil. You can pick the leaves for your cat through the season and then dry them in fall for winter use. To dry, cut the stems before the plant flowers, tie them with a string, and hang them upside down in a cool, dry, shady place. In several weeks the leaves will dry out and you can store them as a treat for Puss during the winter.

GARDENER'S TIP 1
Catnip adapts very well to pot culture, so at the end of the season, pot some and grow it in a sunny window for fresh leaves during the winter.

PESTS: There are none.

VARIETY: Catnip.

SOURCE: Nichols Garden Nursery, 1190 North Pacific Highway, Albany, Oregon 97321.

COOKING TIP 1
After you've satisfied Puss, you can make herbal tea for human consumption. It is best mixed with dried peppermint and lemon balm. Some say it encourages latent tendencies of curiosity.

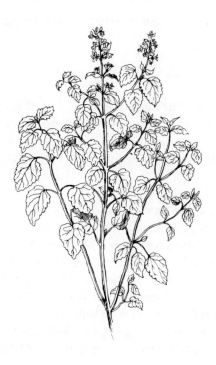

Chervil

*

HARDINESS: Annual, very hardy.

WHEN TO PLANT: In early spring when ground is workable.

SPACING: In rows 1 foot apart, plants 8 inches apart.

DEPTH: 1/8 inch.

HARVEST TIME: 50 to 75 days.

Chervil is relatively unknown in the United States. However, it is used extensively as salad material and in the preparation of elegant sauces on the Continent. It's easily grown if you observe the instructions for germinating difficult seeds. It tastes like a mild tarragon.

HOW TO GROW CHERVIL

Chervil, like parsley, is hardy to cold but sensitive to heat. Therefore, plant early, the same time you plant peas, lettuce, and onions. Full sun, fertile soil, and reasonable moisture are necessary for a fine crop. The trick to growing chervil is the same as that for growing parsley. Germination is slow, and unless you keep your bed well watered, your crop will fail. To overcome this, soak the seeds in water overnight about 2 weeks before planting. After that place the seeds on a damp paper towel, fold the towel up with the contained seeds, and place in the refrigerator until they germinate (about 1 to 2 weeks).

Then sow the seeds thinly in the garden, about 1/8 inch deep, two per inch. After they have grown to a height of about 2 inches, thin them to about 6 inches apart. Pick the leaves as you need them, for others will grow in their place.

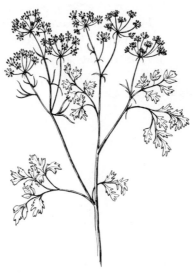

GARDENER'S TIP 1
Chervil can be moved indoors during the winter. Simply pot a plant and place it in a sunny window and enjoy fresh chervil throughout the colder months.

GARDENER'S TIP 2
You can also dry chervil. Pick a supply early in the morning, tie the leaves together with a string, and hang the bundle upside down in a dry, airy place. The leaves should dry out in about 2 weeks. Then crumble the leaves, remove the brittle stems, and store in an airtight container in a cool, dry, dark place.

PESTS: Few, if any.

VARIETY: Simply chervil.

SOURCES: Nichols Garden Nursery, 1190 North Pacific Highway, Albany, Oregon 97321; J. A. Demonchaux Co., 225 Jackon, Topeka, Kansas 66603.

COOKING TIP 1

Many classic French and Belgian fish sauces call for chervil. It is also delicious in soup and salad. Check Nika Hazelton's *The Belgian Cookbook* for an excellent chervil soup recipe.

COOKING TIP 2

In the Provence district of France a very popular salad called *mesclum* is made by mixing the leaves of chervil, arugula, leaf lettuce, and fine-curled endive. In fact, to facilitate picking, the seeds of the four leafy vegetables are mixed together and sowed as one. They are picked at a very, very young stage and prepared with various salad dressings.

Chives

HARDINESS: Perennial, very hardy.

WHEN TO PLANT: In early spring, as soon as ground is workable.

SPACING: In rows 1 foot apart, sow seeds thinly about 1/4 inch apart. Thin to 1 foot.

DEPTH: About 1/4 inch.

HARVEST TIME: Throughout the season.

Chives are very easy to grow. For added pleasure, in the spring, lovely purple flowers adorn the plants. One of the first of all herbs to emerge in the spring, chives add a fresh taste to so many foods. No gourmet should be without this useful herb.

HOW TO GROW CHIVES

Chives are not fussy about soil. Any reasonable fertile soil is suitable. Plant in full sun or semishade. Sow the seeds as early in the spring as ground is workable. Plant thinly, about 1/4 inch apart, 1/4 inch deep. Cover the seeds with fine soil, tamp down, and water gently. In about 2 weeks your seedlings will emerge from the ground. When the plants are about 3 inches high, thin to 1 foot apart. A short row of about 5 feet should provide you with more than enough of this herb. After plants have matured, you can transplant some to your kitchen door area so that they are convenient for picking, as you will find many uses for this member of the onion family. Every few years, dig the plants, divide, and replant.

GARDENER'S TIP 1
If you permit the purple flowers to go to seed, the plant will reseed itself prodigiously. To keep your garden tidy, pick off the flowers before they fade. They are edible and look attractive in a salad bowl.

GARDENER'S TIP 2
In the fall, pick enough chives for winter use. Cut the chives with scissors and freeze for relatively fresh herbs during the winter.

GARDENER'S TIP 3
Chives pot well, so in the fall, dig a small plant, pot it, and place in a sunny windowsill during the winter.

PESTS: Chives are pest-free.

VARIETIES: Simply Chives.

SOURCE: Seed rack at your local garden center.

COOKING TIP 1
Chives combine marvelously with many foods, but a recipe in *The Nouvelle Cuisine of Jean and Pierre Troisgros* for sole with chives is possibly supreme. It consists of lightly sautéed, breaded fish swimming in a delicate, creamy wine sauce, topped with the very subtle onion flavor of chopped chive. It's well worth a look and a try.

COOKING TIP 2
At the Hotel Meridien Copacabana in Rio de Janeiro, Brazil, the restaurants are under the direction of the famous French chef, Paul Bocuse. One of the most appetizing entrées on the menu is a mousse of scallop with a beurre blanc sauce. However, the sauce is not the usual beurre blanc. Consult any basic French cookbook for a fish or shellfish mousse recipe, as well as for a recipe for

beurre blanc sauce. After you have prepared your sauce, add 3 tablespoons of crème fraîche and blend well. Then put the sauce in a blender or food processor and add about 4 teaspoons of chopped chive. Blend until smooth and serve with the mousse.

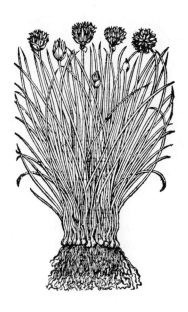

Dill

HARDINESS: Annual, hardy.

WHEN TO PLANT: In early spring, as soon as ground is workable.

SPACING: Sow seed thinly and thin to 3 or 4 inches apart as season progresses.

DEPTH: 1/2 inch.

HARVEST TIME: Throughout the season for fresh dill and at the end of the season for seeds and dried dill weed.

Dill is one of the most versatile herbs grown. It is used widely in the cuisines of Scandinavia, Poland, Hungary, and Czechoslovakia. No gourmet garden should be without this delightful treasure. If you do any pickling at all, you know that dill is basic.

HOW TO GROW DILL

Sow seeds thinly, 1/2 inch deep and thin to about 3 or 4 inches apart during the season. Dill is not fussy about soil and is pest-free, but full sun is required. Keep in mind that this herb, with its feathery leaves, grows to a height of about 2 feet, so plan accordingly in your garden. To protect plants from wind damage you can plant in a circle.

Harvest the leaves as you need them during the season and in the fall be sure to gather seeds for baking and flavoring various dishes. Save some for planting the following spring, but it often self-seeds.

GARDENER'S TIP 1
To dry dill weed, pick a supply early in the morning, tie the leaves with a string, and hang upside down in a dry, shady, airy place. The leaves should dry out in about 2 weeks. Crumble the leaves, removing the brittle stems, and store them in an airtight container in a cool, dry, dark place.

PESTS: There are none.

VARIETY: Dill. Nichols Garden Nursery, 1190 North Pacific Highway, Albany, Oregon 97321, carries a dwarf variety called Dill "Bouquet," if a shorter variety is to your liking.

SOURCE: Seed racks at your local garden center.

COOKING TIP 1
Here's an authentic recipe for making kosher dill pickles: Pack pickling cucumbers as tightly as possible in a quart jar. Add 3 to 4 sprigs dill, 1 large pinch pickling spices, 1 clove garlic, and 1 bay leaf. Fill jars with strong salt water solution (1/3 cup kosher salt to 1 quart water heated until salt dissolves). Cover and let sit at room temperature until pickled to taste. Try after 4 days. If you like stronger pickles let sit a few more days. When desired strength is attained, store in refrigerator. You can also process these pickles.

The Mints

HARDINESS: Perennial, hardy.

WHEN TO PLANT: From early spring to fall.

SPACING: 2 feet apart.

DEPTH: At soil level of purchased stock.

HARVEST TIME: From early spring until plants go to seed or develop woody stalks.

Of course you know what mint is, but did you know that it comes in a wide variety of flavors? The following varieties are available:

Apple mint: An applelike scent and flavor. Grows into a tall, woolly plant.

Lemon mint: As its name implies, a lemony taste.

Orange mint: This has a pleasant orangelike flavor.

Peppermint: The common, tangy mint so well known.

Pineapple mint: One of my favorites, with a mild pineapple scent.

Spearmint: Somewhat strong. Useful if you make your own toothpaste or chewing gum.

HOW TO GROW MINT

Just about infallible, given a minimum of attention. Just plant in sun or shade from spring to fall and water until established. The mints are not fussy about soil.

GARDENER'S TIP 1

All mints should be picked when young. As they grow older, they lose a substantial amount of their delightful taste.

GARDENER'S TIP 2

Mints will run rampant if given a chance. I have found the best way to contain them is to plant them in large plastic tubs and sink the tubs into the soil. Do not let them get out of hand, because if given a chance, they will take over your entire garden within a few years.

GARDENER'S TIP 3

It is best to purchase plants of these mints from mail order houses or nurseries. Undoubtedly, some of your more sophisticated gardener friends raise the more esoteric varieties. Ask them for a snip. Growing from seed can be difficult.

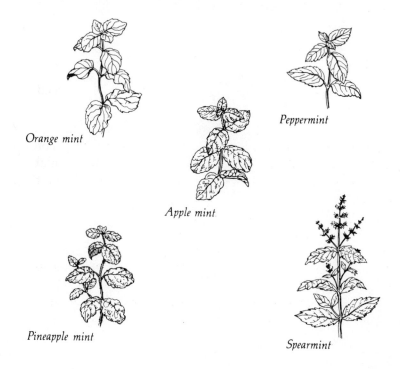

Orange mint

Peppermint

Apple mint

Pineapple mint

Spearmint

PESTS: The mints are subject to several pests and diseases.

VARIETIES: See above.

SOURCE: Nichols Garden Nursery, 1190 North Pacific Highway, Albany, Oregon 97321.

COOKING TIP 1
We all know that mint is a traditional garnish for iced tea, lemonade, and other summer beverages. However, it serves well in hot winter beverages as well. Beyond the mint teas, try adding some dried mint leaves to hot chocolate. It's a very soothing cold-weather delight. And in summer, add fresh mint to cold chocolate. It's delicious in yogurt dressings and in tabouli, the tangy Middle Eastern salad made with bulgur wheat.

Oregano

HARDINESS: Annual.

WHEN TO PLANT: From late spring to early fall.

SPACING: About 2 feet apart.

DEPTH: At soil level of plant.

HARVEST TIME: From late spring to fall.

Oregano is probably best known as the herb which Italians use in spaghetti sauce, pizza, and other dishes. However, you might be surprised to learn that there are many other uses for this versatile herb. For better-flavored oregano, grow your own. There is no comparison between the fresh version and the store-bought product.

HOW TO GROW OREGANO

Your best bet is to purchase plants from a nursery or mail order house. You can grow this herb from seed, but if you do, you will have to start by planting indoors long before the growing season. If you opt for plants, set them in the ground at soil level, about 2 feet apart, after all danger of frost is over, from mid-May to early June.

Plant in full sun and well-drained soil. Aside from that, the needs of oregano are few.

Start picking leaves around the middle of June and continue throughout the summer.

GARDENER'S TIP 1
Oregano has a spreading tendency, so be sure to control your bed.

GARDENER'S TIP 2
Take advantage of the spreading habit and plant in a rock garden, on a slope, or along garden paths.

GARDENER'S TIP 3
Dry some oregano for winter use. Pick early in the day, tie with a string, and hang upside down in a cool, dry, shady place until thoroughly dry. Then remove leaves and discard woody stems, place in airtight containers, and store in a cool, shady, dry place.

PESTS: Oregano is subject to a number of pests and diseases.

VARIETY: Oregano.

SOURCE: Nichols Garden Nursery, 1190 North Pacific Highway, Albany, Oregon 97321.

COOKING TIP 1
Of course, use oregano in Italian cuisine. However, the next time you prepare pot roast, rub the entire piece of meat with fresh or dried oregano. The flavor imparted is delicious. You can do the same thing with roast beef, especially if the strong taste of bay leaf doesn't appeal to you.

Parsley

FRENCH CURLED AND ITALIAN

HARDINESS: Annual, very hardy. Often biennial.

WHEN TO PLANT: In early spring as soon as ground is workable.

SPACING: In rows 1 foot apart, sow seeds thinly.

DEPTH: 1/8 inch.

HARVEST TIME: From 50 to 75 days.

There are two kinds of parsley used in the preparation of gourmet foods. French curled parsley is used primarily for garnish, although it can be used in cooking or salad. The Italian or broadleafed parsley is said to be far more intense in flavor and is consequently used more commonly in gourmet cooking. Both are easily grown if you know the simple trick of speeding up seed germination.

HOW TO GROW PARSLEY
Parsley is hardy to cold but sensitive to heat. It thrives on conditions similar to those for growing kale, lettuce, and spinach. And, if given a little protection, you can often carry it over the winter, affording fresh parsley leaves very early in the spring.

Parsley thrives in any good soil. Cut during the early stages of its growth, it is very delicate, so a finely powdered, friable soil is preferable. The most common problem with failure of a parsley crop involves the germination of the tiny seeds. They are extremely slow in germinating, sometimes taking more than a month. The secret to success is to put them in the freezer for a few days, then soak the seeds in water overnight about 1 week before planting time. After that, place the seeds on a damp paper towel, fold the towel up with the contained seeds, place in a plastic sandwich bag, and put in the refrigerator. After about a week, the tiny seeds will germinate and you can plant them directly in your garden.

Sow thinly, six seeds per inch, about 1/8 inch deep in full sun. When the plants are 2 to 3 inches high, thin them to 6 inches apart. Pick the leaves as you need them, for others will grow in their place.

GARDENER'S TIP 1
You can plant a crop of parsley in the fall, mulch it heavily to protect from the extreme cold of winter, and then in spring remove mulch.

GARDENER'S TIP 2
For a continuous supply of parsley during the winter, dig a plant, pot it, and place it on a sunny windowsill. Your parsley should thrive. If you have a cat, you might find that she will nibble at your plant, so provide some sort of protection.

PESTS: Depending on your locality, parsleyworm can be a problem.

VARIETIES: Extra Curled Dwarf is the French variety; Plain or Single is the Italian.

SOURCE: Most mail order nurseries and seed rack at your local garden center.

COOKING TIP 1
In addition to using parsley as garnish and in cooking, many Continental cooks lightly French-fry parsley in oil and serve it with fish or vegetables. Simply place a handful of stalks in hot oil for a few seconds, remove, drain, and serve immediately. This will add a very elegant touch to your entrées.

Rosemary

HARDINESS: Perennial in the South and, with protection in the winter, sometimes perennial in the North. To be sure of a crop, grow as an annual in the North.

WHEN TO PLANT: In spring after all danger of frost, from mid-May to early June.

SPACING: Sow sparsely and thin to 6 to 8 inches apart when 2 inches high.

DEPTH: 1/2 inch.

HARVEST TIME: Fresh during the season and for drying in the fall.

Another of the staple herbs for gourmet cooking, rosemary is used in many classic dishes made with lamb and chicken.

HOW TO GROW ROSEMARY

Plant in spring when all danger of frost is over, from mid-May to early June. Sow seeds thinly, 1/2 inch deep, and when plants are 2 inches high, thin to 6 to 8 inches apart. Rosemary is not fussy about soil, but reasonable sunshine is a requirement. The plant is handsome, resembling a small pine tree. Harvest throughout the season as needed or cut and dry in the fall. Tie in bunches and hang upside down in a cool, shady, dry place to dry. After 2 weeks or so, when thoroughly dry, store in airtight containers in a cool, dry, dark place.

GARDENER'S TIP 1
Rosemary can be incorporated into a border or flower bed, for its decorative foliage and lovely blue flowers are very attractive.

GARDENER'S TIP 2
If you live in the North and wish to try to winter over this plant, locate it near a south wall or in a sheltered spot, or pot up and bring inside. Mulch heavily after the first killing frost and you will probably succeed.

PESTS: Rosemary is subject to a number of pests and diseases.

VARIETY: Rosemary, There is also a prostrate variety available.

SOURCE: Most garden centers and mail order houses carry seeds of this plant, and many nurseries purvey plants.

COOKING TIP 1
You can turn plain old breaded zucchini or eggplant into something special by adding about 1 teaspoon crushed rosemary leaves to 1 cup bread crumbs.

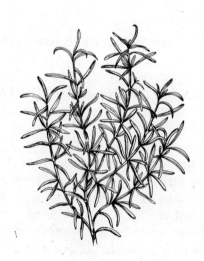

Sage

◯

HARDINESS: Perennial, hardy.

WHEN TO PLANT: In early spring, as soon as ground is workable.

SPACING: Set plants about 2 feet apart.

DEPTH: Plant to soil line on stock.

HARVEST TIME: Throughout season when needed and in fall for drying.

Sage is another of the staple herbs used in cooking, both "gourmet" and "plain." Again, as with all herbs, the home-grown fresh variety is far superior to the dried versions available in the markets. Sage dries well for winter use.

HOW TO GROW SAGE

Purchase plants from a nursery or reliable mail order house. Sage is not fussy about soil, though it prefers well-drained loam. Plant your sage in full sun, giving it plenty of space. Cultivate during the season to keep weed-free, and water during extreme dry spells. You won't be able to harvest a substantial amount of this herb until the third year or so, but once mature, a generous supply will be available to you all during the season. Harvest

fresh leaves throughout the season and pick a supply to dry for
winter use.

GARDENER'S TIP 1
Sage tends to be invasive, so be sure to keep your plants in
bounds. You can plant your sage in a plastic tub and sink it into
the ground.

GARDENER'S TIP 2
You can divide your plants every few years should you need a
larger supply. Dig the plant in the spring, divide it into two or
three separate plants, and replant.

GARDENER'S TIP 3
To dry, pick early in the morning in the early fall, tie leaves
together, and hang upside down in a cool, airy, shaded place until
dry. Then store in airtight containers in a cool, dark, dry place.

GARDENER'S TIP 4
Avoid pineapple sage. It is attractive to the eye, but has little or
no flavor.

PESTS: Sage is subject to a number of pests and diseases.

VARIETIES:
 Dwarf Vatican Sage: This miniature traces its origins to the
Vatican gardens.
 Emperor Sage: A large plant with deep purple leaves.
 Holt's Mammoth Sage: This is the best sage for flavor. It is
grown commercially.
 Red Tricolor Sage: This has a white pointed leaf with red and
purple coloration.

SOURCE: Nichols Garden Nursery, 1190 North Pacific Highway, Albany, Oregon 97321.

COOKING TIP 1
Sage is good with pork or beef and in jellies and teas.

Sesame Seed

HARDINESS: Annual, tender.

WHEN TO PLANT: After all danger of frost, from mid-May to early June.

SPACING: Plant 1 inch apart and thin to 6 inches apart when seedlings are 2 inches high.

DEPTH: 1/4 inch.

HARVEST TIME: In the fall when flowers have dried, but before seed pods burst.

Sesame seed is the oldest known oil-producing seed grown by man. Its cultivation is recorded in China in 3000 B.C., and the Egyptians grew it before Moses' time. There has always been a mysterious aura surrounding the seed, and yes, the magic words, "Open sesame," uttered by Ali Baba in "Ali Baba and the Forty Thieves" refers to this seed. You can grow it easily in your own garden.

HOW TO GROW SESAME SEED
Wait until the soil warms thoroughly and plant the seed 1 inch apart, 1/4 inch deep, in full sun. Thin to 6 inches apart when seedlings are 2 inches high. As the plant grows it will reach a

height of from 2 to 9 feet, depending on growing conditions. One to three flowers will grow on the leaf axils from pods which are gathered for the crop. Keep weeded and watered during the summer. When flowers have dried, pick them off and harvest the seeds. Store in airtight containers in a cool, dry, dark place.

GARDENER'S TIP 1
For best results, plant your seeds along a south wall, as sesame needs long hot days of sun and warm nights. Do not attempt to grow this plant in the far northern reaches of the country.

GARDENER'S TIP 2
Mr. Philip Haralambou, a retired gentleman who is a native of the beautiful island of Cyprus and a friend and neighbor, told me that in Cyprus, people harvest the flowers just before they are completely dry and then place them on a sheet in the sun to dry. You would do well to follow his advice, as when sesame pods are ripe, they pop open and scatter the seeds.

PESTS: There are none.

VARIETY: Sesame.

SOURCE: Nichols Garden Nursery, 1190 North Pacific Highway, Albany, Oregon 97321.

COOKING TIP 1
Once you've developed an addiction to sesame seeds, like garlic, you'll find an excuse to add them to almost anything. However, you've probably never thought of adding them to creamed spinach or Swiss chard. It's a simple trick, but the nutty flavor added to the vegetable is terrific.

Tarragon

HARDINESS: Perennial, hardy.

WHEN TO PLANT: After all danger of frost, from mid-May to early June.

SPACING: Depending on growing conditions, 1 to 2 feet apart.

DEPTH: Soil line of plant.

HARVEST TIME: Throughout the season from late spring to late fall.

Tarragon is somewhat difficult to grow. First of all, most varieties which are available in nurseries are not the genuine French article. Another problem with tarragon is that its needs in terms of soil are minimal. If you grow this herb in rich soil, it will probably die. Since it is a native of the Mediterranean area, poor soil, full sun, and some moisture are required for best results. This herb seems to grow especially well in seacoast areas of this country. In addition, growing from seed is also difficult. Your best bet will be to order a *French* tarragon from a reputable nursery.

HOW TO GROW TARRAGON
Select a sunny spot and plant your stock at the soil level at which it grew in the nursery. Plant in poor soil, preferably rocky. Ideally

this plant will grow to 2 to 3 feet tall, almost like a small shrub. Set your plants about 2 feet apart. Water during extreme dry spells. Harvest leaves throughout the season and dry some for winter use.

GARDENER'S TIP 1
To dry, pick stalks early in the morning, tie them up, and hang upside down in a cool, shady, dry place. When dry, about 2 to 3 weeks later, remove the leaves from the stalks, store in airtight containers, and place in a cool, dark, dry place.

PESTS: Tarragon is virtually disease- and pest-free.

VARIETY: French tarragon. All others are a far cry from the genuine article.

SOURCE: Nichols Garden Nursery, 1190 North Pacific Highway, Albany, Oregon 97321.

COOKING TIP 1
To make tarragon vinegar, simply place about six sprigs of tarragon leaves in a pint jar of white vinegar. Cover and allow to steep for several months. Use as needed. Once steeped, do not remove the leaves from the jar. Tarragon vinegar will keep indefinitely.

The Thymes

HARDINESS: Perennial, hardy.

WHEN TO PLANT: From early spring through midsummer.

SPACING: Set plants about 2 feet apart.

DEPTH: Plant at soil line on stock.

HARVEST TIME: Throughout the season when needed and into fall for drying.

Thyme is a staple in all cooking, both gourmet domestic and gourmet foreign. The home-grown fresh variety is infinitely superior to commercial versions. Like mints, thyme is available in a variety of flavors, as well as in different growth habits. Varieties are:

Creeping Caraway-Scented Thyme: If caraway seeds get stuck in your teeth or dentures, this variety should appeal to you.

Creeping Red Thyme: A dwarf creeping variety covered with purplish red flowers. It is strongly scented.

Creeping White Moss Thyme: Emerald green, a matlike grower with tiny white flowers. This is mildly scented.

English Thyme: The common thyme commercially grown.

French Thyme: That preferred by French chefs. The flavor is considerably more subtle and the leaves are narrow and daintier.

Lemon Thyme: Lemon-scented leaves that make good herbal tea.

HOW TO GROW THYME

Plant your stock in a sunny spot. Any type of soil will suffice. Thyme is native to the Mediterranean area where sun shines, rain doesn't fall, and soil is poor. Once established, the plants are virtually indestructible and will grow more beautiful with each passing year.

GARDENER'S TIP 1

For a poetic experience, plant the creeping varieties, Creeping Red and Creeping White Moss, between bricks or flagstones on your patio or in garden paths. As you walk over the plants and bruise them, the scent of thyme will fill the air.

GARDENER'S TIP 2

To dry for winter, cut the stalks before they flower, wash to remove dirt and insects, tie them together, and hang them upside down in a cool, dry, shady place. When they have dried, after several weeks, remove the leaves and store in airtight containers in a cool, dry place until ready to use. Your herbs will have a more pungent taste if you grind the leaves to a powdery consistency as you use them.

GARDENER'S TIP 3
Be sure not to overwater thyme. If you do, it will die.

PESTS: There are none.

VARIETIES: All of the above.

SOURCE: Nichols Garden Nursery, 1190 North Pacific Highway, Albany, Oregon 97321, has the best selection.

COOKING TIP 1:
Use thyme in chowders, teas, salads. This herb is also an excellent complement to green beans.

Berries

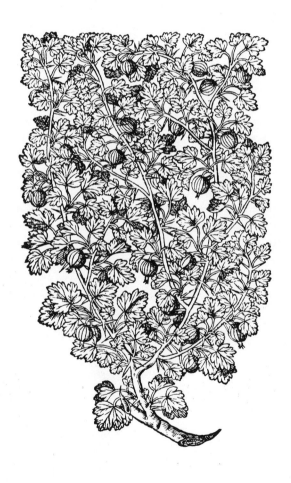

There are three good reasons for growing your own berries. First, fresh home-grown berries are always superior in taste and quality to anything you can purchase in the markets. Second, more often than not, most varieties of berries are simply not available unless you grow them yourself. The reason for this is they are very perishable and do not ship well. And third, if they are available, they are usually outrageously expensive.

Just think of having more raspberries at your disposal than you can use! This luxury can be yours with a minimum investment of time, money, and space.

Blackberries

HARDINESS: Hardy perennial.

WHEN TO PLANT: In spring, as soon as the ground is workable.

SPACING: In rows 7 to 8 feet apart, with plants about 3 to 5 feet apart.

DEPTH: Soil line of stock.

HARVEST TIME: In early and midsummer when berries are ripe.

Fresh blackberries are rarely available in the markets. So, if you enjoy these delicious morsels you must grow your own in your garden. There is nothing complicated about growing blackberries, but keep your patch contained, as blackberries have a tendency to spread.

HOW TO GROW BLACKBERRIES

Order your stock from a mail order nursery, as few local garden centers stock this variety of berry. There are two types of black-berries: those which trail and those which grow erect. The trailing types are not fully hardy in the most northerly states and need support when they grow. If you do not provide this, your patch will become an ugly, unmanageable mess. Unless you are prepared for this extra work, and have lots of space, you would do well to purchase only the erect varieties. This variety develops arched canes which are self-supporting.

Blackberries are not fussy about soil as long as moisture is abundant. Ideally, sandy loam with a good supply of humus worked in is most to their liking. Keep in mind when locating your patch that you will need access to a supply of water, as blackberries need a lot of moisture during the period when the berries are developing.

Prepare the soil by adding several bushels of rotted manure for each 50-foot row. Or, if you wish, you can work in 3 to 4 pounds of 5-10-5 fertilizer or 6 to 8 pounds of organic mixture. Cultivate to keep weeds free, and water copiously during berry set and hot summer months.

HOW TO THIN BLACKBERRY CANES

The new canes which grow from your plants will live for only 2 years, so they must be cut out at the end of each season. Keep in mind that the new canes produce side shoots the first year, and during the second year, these side shoots throw blossoms which ripen into fruit. Once the cane has fruited, it dies.

HOW TO PRUNE BLACKBERRIES

A certain amount of pruning is necessary if you want a bumper harvest of large berries. In the fall of the first year, the new stalks will have sent out side branches. These are called laterals. Cut these back to from four to six buds on each lateral.

WHEN TO HARVEST

Blackberries ripen in early to midsummer. When they are ready to eat, they will be firm and sweet. Do not let them get soft and overripe.

GARDENER'S TIP 1

In colder regions, you will have to protect your creeping plants. At the end of the season untie, bend over the canes to the ground, and cover them with a layer of earth, compost, or hay. Then in the spring, when the weather warms up, uncover them.

PESTS: Blackberries are reasonably resistant to insect invasions. Keep your patch clean by removing old canes and any patches of wild raspberries or wild blackberries which might be nearby. Diseases often start in the wild patches and then move on to your more sophisticated plants.

VARIETIES: Darrow and Thornfree (this is less prolific but has the advantage of having no thorns). Black Satin is carried by Park Seed and is also thorn-free.

SOURCES: W. Atlee Burpee Co., Warminster, Pennsylvania 18974, or Clinton, Iowa 52732; George W. Park Seed Co., Greenwood, South Carolina 29647.

COOKING TIP 1:
A favorite of mine is cold blackberry soup. Wash and pick over 1 pound of ripe blackberries. Put in a saucepan with 1 lemon, thinly sliced, 2 cups cold water, a 1-inch stick of cinnamon, 2 cloves, and 1/2 cup granulated sugar. Bring to a boil, lower the flame, and simmer gently for 10 minutes or until the fruit is soft. Rub through a fine sieve and chill well. Just before serving, stir in 2 cups chilled sour cream. You can also use wild blackberries to make this soup.

Blueberries

HARDINESS: Shrubby perennial, hardy.

WHEN TO PLANT: In early spring, while dormant.

SPACING: 3 to 8 feet apart, in rows 5 to 8 feet apart.

DEPTH: At soil level of stock.

HARVEST TIME: From early summer to late summer, depending on variety.

Although blueberries are usually available in the market, they are such handsome and hardy plants that you should consider growing them in your garden. If you select a range of varieties from early to late bearing, you will have a continuous supply of these delicious berries all summer.

HOW TO GROW BLUEBERRIES

Perhaps the most important thing you must keep in mind when planting your blueberry bushes is that these berries require an acid soil. If you do not know whether or not the soil in your area is acidic, inquire of neighbors or local nursery people. Beyond that, you can always purchase an inexpensive soil testing kit to determine whether or not you will have to take steps to correct the acidic composition of your planting area. A pH of 4.0 to 4.8

is best, although some people have luck with these plants when the pH is as high as 5.0. If your pH is higher than that, you may have to add sulfate of ammonia to your soil regularly in order to maintain the proper acidity. If you find that azalea and rhododendron thrive in your garden, blueberries probably will as well.

To help your plants get a good start, dig deep holes and mix in a considerable amount of peat moss, rotted manure, and compost. At the same time, once you have determined the pH of your soil, add sulfate of ammonia as indicated by a soil test.

You can purchase your blueberry plants from a local nursery. However, the range of varieties will probably be limited. Keep in mind that it is advisable to plant two or more different varieties in order to secure maximum cross-pollination. A good idea is to select stock from early, midseason, and late-bearing varieties. Order from a reliable mail order house, as they almost always have a reasonable selection. But be sure to order early, as generally supplies are limited. If possible, order two- or three-year-old plants.

When your plants arrive, plant them at the level at which they grew in the nursery. Water thoroughly and mulch the soil around the plants with 3 or 4 inches of acidic peat moss, sawdust, or wood chips. Remove all fruit buds the first year, so that the plant's energy will be directed to root growth.

During droughts water at least 1 inch a week and keep weeds at a minimum by cultivating. Do not cultivate too deeply or you will disturb surface roots.

HOW TO PRUNE BLUEBERRY BUSHES
For larger berries, although smaller yield, prune your bushes lightly. Remove the small, slender branches and leave the strong vigorous shoots. These will always produce the largest berries. Prune in early spring when plant is still dormant. As the bush grows, be sure to "open it up," that is, remove some of the inner branches so that air circulation and sunlight are permitted to aid your plants in their productivity.

GARDENER'S TIP 1
A full-grown blueberry bush should produce from 8 to 10 quarts of berries per year.

GARDENER'S TIP 2
You must net these bushes to protect the fruit from the birds.

GARDENER'S TIP 3
Blueberries are handsome plants and can be incorporated into your landscape design. In May, pinkish white flowers appear, followed by fruit, and in the fall the leaves turn red. In winter the red and green twigs and red buds are attractive.

PESTS: There are few, if any, except birds.

VARIETIES: In order of ripening: Earliblue, Blueray, Atlantic, Jersey, Burlington, Coville.

SOURCE: Henry Leuthardt Nurseries, Inc., Montauk Highway, East Moriches, New York 11940.

VARIETIES: Bluecrop, Blueray.

SOURCE: Stark Brothers Nurseries, Louisiana, Missouri 63353.

VARIETIES: Elliot, Patriot, and some of above.

SOURCE: W. Atlee Burpee Co., Warminster, Pennsylvania 18974 or Clinton, Iowa 52732.

COOKING TIP 1
A blueberry pie with uncooked fresh berries is much more to my taste than one using cooked or baked berries. Here's a recipe that I use. You can do the same thing with fresh peaches, strawberries, or any other very fresh and ripe fruit or berry. Use your favorite pie crust recipe and make a 9-inch pie crust. Be sure to prick the bottom of the crust with a fork. Bake and set aside. In a 2-quart pot put 1 1/3 cups sugar and 1/2 cup water. Bring to a boil and reduce heat. Then dissolve 1/4 cup cornstarch in 3/4 cup water. Add to sugar water and cook about 10 minutes, stirring constantly, until the mixture is clear. Cool and add 1 tablespoon lemon juice and 1/8 teaspoon salt. Add to fresh fruit or berries and mix gently. When mixture is completely cool, place in baked pie crust. Serve with whipped cream.

If you use fresh peaches or strawberries for this pie, reduce sugar to 3/4 cup and water to 1/4 cup. Dissolve cornstarch in 1/2 cup water. Add vanilla or almond extract to the fresh peaches if you make a peach pie.

Currants

BLACK

These are the berries which the French use to make cassis, the delicious sweet syrup used in mixed drinks and spritzers. However, you never see plants of this variety advertised in the catalogs of major American nurseries. The reason is that at the present time, there is a ban on selling and growing black currants in most of the United States because they are alternate host plants for blister rust disease, a deadly fungus that attacks and kills white pine trees.

There are no restrictions against planting this variety in the following states: Alabama, Alaska, Arkansas, Florida, Kansas, Louisiana, Mississippi, Missouri, Nebraska, North and South Dakota, Oklahoma, Texas, and Hawaii. If you reside in one of these states, stock is probably available from a local nursery. Do not under any circumstances export them to your home state if you reside in restricted areas. The resultant disease and death of white pine will wreak havoc with the environment.

However, hope springs eternal, for a new variety of black currant has been developed in Canada which is resistant to white pine blister rust. It will be available in the United States within the next year or so. For further information contact Kelly Brothers Nursery, Dansville, New York 14437. I'd advise you to inquire now, as stock will be very limited when first available.

Cultivation of black currants is the same as for the red variety, so consult the following section on red currants for instructions.

Currants

RED

🖋

HARDINESS: Shrubby perennial, hardy.

WHEN TO PLANT: Early spring before dormancy is broken.

SPACING: About 5 feet apart.

DEPTH: At soil line of stock.

HARVEST TIME: Early to midseason, depending on variety.

Where would a discriminating cook be without currant jelly to use as a glaze on meats, poultry, and pastry? Currants are easily grown, are not fussy about soil, and will thrive in semishade or sun. This coupled with the fact that the bushes are attractive— coordinate them in your landscape scheme.

HOW TO GROW CURRANTS
Order your plants from a reliable mail order house or purchase them at your local nursery. Keep in mind that most local nurseries do not stock this plant, so if you wish to include them in your garden, inquire early so that you can order by mail if necessary. Currants grow readily in most soils, from clay loam to heavy clay. The one kind of soil they do not like is sandy soil. If that is your soil condition, plant your bushes in a well-shaded spot, even on the north side of your house.

Dig a good-size hole, spread the roots out over a cone of earth, and fill in with soil. Water thoroughly.

Mulch your bushes heavily. This will help keep the soil cool, retain moisture, and eliminate the need for cultivation which might damage the surface roots. In addition, the mulch will provide nutrients for the soil as it decomposes.

Each spring, before you apply the mulch, put about 1 inch of compost or rotted manure on the surface of the soil. Water during droughts.

Currants bear on year-old wood and at the bottom of older wood, so you must prune your bushes each fall after the plants go dormant. The recommended practice is to prune out all three-year-old wood. You can also pinch back new growth in late spring in order to foster leaf cover and new growth.

GARDENER'S TIP 1

Propagating currants is easy. In the fall, after the leaves begin to drop, cut wood from strong, healthy plants. Select the thickest branches. Cut the tops straight across and the bottoms at any angle. In this way, you'll be able to tell which end is the top and which end is the bottom. The cuttings should be about 10 to 12 inches long. Tie the cuttings in a bundle, dig a pit, place the cuttings at the bottom, and cover them. In the spring, dig them up and plant them, bottom end down. They will have healthy roots on them by that time.

GARDENER'S TIP 2

Birds relish currants, so if you want any left for yourself, you will have to net your entire stand of bushes. Be sure to follow this advice. If you don't, you will not have one single berry left on your bushes.

PESTS: Currants are pest-free, except for birds.

VARIETIES: Cherry, an early variety; Diploma, which has the reputation of being best for jelly and syrup; Perfection, for good table eating; and Red Lake, a midseason variety.

SOURCE: George W. Park Seed Co. Inc., Greenwood, South Carolina 29647.

COOKING TIP 1

To make an excellent syrup follow these instructions: In a gallon jug place 4 quarts of berries. (This recipe can be used to make raspberry or strawberry syrup as well.) Let stand in the sun for 4 days. Be sure to cover the jar with about five or six layers of cheesecloth. Extract the juice from the berries by squeezing them in the jar. Strain and place in a saucepan with 4 cups sugar. Cook about 6 minutes or just to the boiling point. Pour into hot sterilized jars and process. If a few fruit flies should find their way through the cheesecloth into the juice, merely pick or strain them out. They are harmless.

Fraises des Bois

ALPINE STRAWBERRIES

HARDINESS: Perennial, hardy.

WHEN TO PLANT: In early spring, as soon as ground is workable.

SPACING: About 1 foot apart.

DEPTH: Where crown meets root system.

HARVEST TIME: All during the season as berries ripen.

Undoubtedly, if you have visited the finer restaurants of Belgium and France, you've probably seen these berries on menus and perhaps have even ordered and savored them. Classically, they are served with clotted cream or crème fraîche. They are available in this country at posh food emporiums, but prices are exorbitant because they are flown over fresh from Europe. Once you've planted your stock, each year you can triple or quadruple your plants by dividing, so although the initial outlay may be more than you'd care to spend, in the long run, these plants are very inexpensive. They run about $24 a dozen. There are no tricks to growing fraises des bois—in fact, they are more easily grown than our own very delicious cultivated varieties.

HOW TO GROW FRAISES DES BOIS

Order plants from a reliable nursery and set in the ground in very early spring, as soon as the ground is workable. If plants arrive with two or three crowns per specimen, separate them into individual plants and set in ground at crown level. There are no special soil needs for fraises des bois, and they seem to thrive in either full sun or partial shade *if* they are kept well watered.

You can also plant fraises des bois from seed. Sow indoors from January to May. After hardening off in midspring, set outdoors in permanent spot.

GARDENER'S TIP 1

These plants do not send out runners as do our domestic varieties, so you can use them quite effectively as a border for a perennial bed or for lining a walk.

GARDENER'S TIP 2

Each spring dig up your plants and divide them into individual crowns and replant. Be sure to do this very early, before the leaves have unfolded.

GARDENER'S TIP 3

Fraises des bois bear fruit all through the season, until frost and beyond.

GARDENER'S TIP 4

If you wish, you can grow many varieties of fraises des bois from seed. Most mail order houses carry this berry under the name of Alpine strawberries, but they are not the same berry as those carried by White Flower Farm.

PESTS: There are none.

VARIETIES: Charles V is the French variety.

SOURCE FOR PLANTS: White Flower Farm, Litchfield, Connecticut 06759.

VARIETIES: Alpine yellow fruited, Alexandria, Baron Solemacher, Rugen Improved.

SOURCES FOR SEEDS: George W. Park Seed Co., Inc. Green-wood, South Carolina 29647; W. Atlee Burpee Co., Warminster, Pennsylvania 18974 or Clinton, Iowa 52732.

COOKING TIP 1

In France, fraises des bois are served with *Coeur à la Crème* made in heart-shaped containers, or with crème fraîche. A reasonable facsimile of the European product can be made at home by combining 2 cups heavy cream with 1/2 tablespoon buttermilk. Simply pour 1 1/2 cups heavy cream into a Mason jar, then add the buttermilk and the rest of the cream. Screw the lid on loosely and let sit at room temperature for 14 to 18 hours. This time can vary depending on temperature. In summer the crème fraîche can thicken in 8 hours; in winter, it may take 24 hours. When thick, tighten the lid and refrigerate. Fill a container with crème fraîche and top with the tiny berries.

Gooseberries

⟋

HARDINESS: Shrubby perennial, hardy.

WHEN TO PLANT: Early spring, before dormancy is broken.

SPACING: About 4 feet apart.

DEPTH: At soil line on stock.

HARVEST TIME: Midsummer, when fruit has turned from light green to plum color.

Gooseberries are an old-fashioned berry that is rarely available in the markets. Delicious tarts, pies, and an unforgettable jam are made from them. They are virtually maintenance-free and are attractive plants that can be incorporated into your landscape design.

HOW TO GROW GOOSEBERRIES

Your best bet is to order from a mail order nursery, as local garden centers rarely carry stock of this berry. Gooseberries are not fussy about soil and will grow in most earth from clay loam to heavy clay. They will tolerate semishade, so a northern or western exposure is satisfactory. When your plants arrive, dig a good-size hole, spread the roots out over a cone of earth, and fill with soil. Water thoroughly. Mulch your plants with several inches of compost in order to preserve moisture, keep the surface roots cool, and eliminate the need for cultivation. The mulch will add nutrients to the soil as it decomposes.

Every year or so, at the end of the season, cut out the older canes to keep your plant vigorous. You can also pinch back new growth in late spring, to force new shoots and branching. This will result in a larger crop of berries.

GARDENER'S TIP 1

Propagating gooseberry bushes is a simple matter. Simply bend one of the branches to the ground, cover a portion of the branch with soil, and place a brick or stone on top of it. In a year or two, roots will have formed and you can cut your new plant free from the parent and set it in the soil.

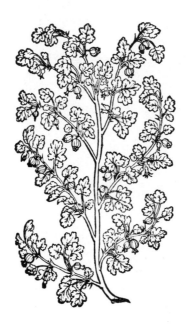

GARDENER'S TIP 2

If you have a problem with birds eating the berries, and I never have, simply net the plants when the fruit forms.

PESTS: Gooseberries, like currants, are subject to pine blister rust. In some areas of the United States where white pine trees grow, it is illegal to plant gooseberries. Check with your County

Extension Agent as to whether or not you live in a prohibited area.

Occasionally scale or borers may attack your plant. If you spot scale, spray with dormant oil spray in early spring. If borers are present, and you can tell if you see little piles of sawdust material on or near the branches, cut off the infected branches and burn or dispose of them.

VARIETY: Pixwell Gooseberry.

SOURCE: Geo. W. Park Co., Inc., Greenwood, South Carolina 29647.

COOKING TIP 1
Before you prepare gooseberries for eating and cooking, snip off the tiny little stems that form on the end of each berry. Beyond the classic gooseberry pies and tarts so favored on the Continent, and of course, the very special gooseberry jam, these luscious small fruits can be spiced and served with duck, chicken, or other fowl as you would a cranberry sauce. See *The Spice Cookbook* by Avanelle Day and Lillie Stuckey for an interesting recipe.

Raspberries

RED

HARDINESS: Hardy, but sensitive to cold in far northern areas.

WHEN TO PLANT: Early spring, as soon as ground is workable.

SPACING: In rows 5 to 8 feet apart, plants 2 to 3 feet apart.

DEPTH: Slightly below soil line on stock.

HARVEST TIME: In early summer and again in the fall if you select ever-bearing varieties.

The reasons why red raspberries are so outrageously expensive in the markets are twofold. First, they must be picked by hand, which means high labor costs. Second, the berries are very perishable and must be shipped to market almost immediately after picking in order to reach customers in an edible state. In fact, even with modern refrigeration, the time from picking to table probably shouldn't be any longer than 2 days. There is nothing difficult about raising your own raspberries. Once established, a bed will provide enough for your table, preserving, and other delectable treats.

HOW TO GROW RED RASPBERRIES
A rich, friable soil is a prerequisite for growing red raspberries, so if your soil is not up to par, fortify it with generous amounts

of rotted manure, compost, and peat moss. The reason is that these delectable berries need plenty of moisture to develop properly and the improved soil will retain the moisture better. Plan on at least a bushel of organic fortification for every six plants.

Once you've established ideal soil conditions, purchase your plants. You have two alternatives. Either order them by mail from reliable seed houses or buy them at your local garden center. But, and most important, buy only virus-free, healthy plants. There are two distinct kinds of raspberries: those that bear part of their crop in the fall and the balance in late spring or early summer and those that bear in July on the previous year's growth. The first kind are called "ever-bearing" and I recommend them highly.

After your plants have arrived, get them into the ground as soon as possible. If the roots are a little dry, soak them in a pail of water for an hour or two before planting. Red raspberries should be set into the ground about 1 inch below nursery level. Plant them 2 to 3 feet apart, in rows from 5 to 8 feet apart. Cultivate to remove weeds, but be careful not to injure the new shoots or surface roots. Provide plenty of water during the first season of growth.

HOW TO PRUNE RED RASPBERRIES
After planting, there is a moderate amount of yearly maintenance involved in the cultivation of raspberries. First keep in mind that

the ever-bearing varieties will produce two crops a year: one in the fall and one in June or July. The July crop bears on last year's growth in both kinds of berries. Once it has produced a crop, the canes die. In the meantime, at the base of each plant the new canes which will produce the fall crop in the case of "ever-bearers" and the subsequent July crop will begin to grow. This means that each year the old canes must be removed. You can do this either after you have picked the July crop or in late fall, when the plants go into dormancy. I have found it an easier task to remove the spent and now dead canes in the fall. You will have no difficulty in distinguishing between the old canes and the new September canes.

Beyond that, each fall, head back the canes by cutting them back to 3 feet. In the case of the full-croffers wait until the fruiting is over. Cut them back to 36 inches. In this way, each plant will branch in the spring and produce a more abundant crop.

GARDENER'S TIP 1
Raspberries ripen rapidly at harvest time. When your berries are bright red and part easily from the stem, it is time to pick. Daily picking is necessary, as these perishable berries deteriorate on the canes once ripe. Excess berries may be frozen readily. Simply place the berries in airtight containers and put them in the freezer. Use these later to make jelly, jam, or syrup.

GARDENER'S TIP 2
Keep your raspberry patch contained. You will notice new shoots emerging from the ground as far away as 6 or 8 feet from your patch. Dig them out, then plant them elsewhere, give them to friends or neighbors, or dispose of them.

GARDENER'S TIP 3
When you install your raspberries, be absolutely certain you have access to both sides of each row. This will facilitate maintenance and harvesting. I plant mine in a single row. Do not plant your patch along a fence, wall, or shrub border, if you can help it.

PESTS: Virus diseases pose the greatest problems, and prevention is the best cure. Be sure to purchase plants only from reliable nurseries or mail order houses. Keep the patch weed-free, and cut out all old or diseased canes. If a virus problem emerges, the only solution is to start a new bed, choosing a different section of your garden for it, or if this is impossible, wait several years before replanting.

Occasionally raspberry crown borer may strike. These are white, grublike larvae which burrow into bark at the plant's base. A 25 percent Diazinon EC solution should be used to drench crowns and lower canes around the latter part of the growing season. Repeat this again 2 weeks later. Do not use this chemical if fruit is on the plant.

VARIETY: I recommend Heritage Everbearing.

SOURCE: Most mail order houses and many garden centers.

COOKING TIP 1

After your bed is established, you will have a bumper crop. Here are some ideas as to what to do with the surfeit. Try making raspberry jelly instead of jam. There are no pits to make the taste bitter. Follow instructions for syrup included in section on currants. But here is a triumph you might want to try: In the past few years, vinaigre de framboise (raspberry vinegar) has become very popular with sophisticated cooks. The only problem is that it costs anywhere from $10 to $15 a pint in specialty stores. You can make it at home for the cost of a bottle of white vinegar if you have a supply of fresh raspberries.

Simply fill a 2-quart jar with fresh raspberries and then pour in enough white vinegar to cover. Cover the top of the jar with about five thicknesses of cheesecloth and tie securely or fasten with a rubber band.

Place the jar in a sunny window for about 4 or 5 weeks. At the end of that time, the berries will have turned white and the vinegar a deep wine red. Remove the cheesecloth and strain the mixture first through a kitchen sieve, and then through several layers of cheesecloth. If any fruit flies find their way through the cheesecloth covering during the brewing stage, just pick them out. Bottle the vinegar, cover, and place in the refrigerator. It will keep indefinitely.

COOKING TIP 2

Now what do you do with raspberry vinegar? First you can use it in dressings for shellfish salads in place of white wine or cider vinegar. It imparts a delicate, fruity taste to the salad.

My favorite use for this ruby delight is to make a sauce for liver, kidney, or other organ meats. While in Belgium, Count Peter Esterhazy, the distinguished photographer, wine expert, and gourmand, told me how to do it. Simply sauté calves' liver (or for that matter, deveined beef liver) in butter. When it is nicely browned, but still pink inside, remove it from the frying pan and keep warm in the oven. Then pour about 1/3 cup raspberry vinegar into the frying pan and mix it with the browned butter and pan juices. As you bring it to a boil you'll notice the heady, piquant aroma. Reduce it very slightly, pour over the meat, and serve. You won't believe how utterly delicious plain old liver tastes when prepared in this manner. You can also fix veal kidneys in the same way. Once you've tasted both of these, you'll find yourself experimenting to find other uses for this treat.

Raspberries

BLACK AND YELLOW

HARDINESS: Hardy, but sensitive to cold in far northern areas.

WHEN TO PLANT: Spring.

SPACING: Rows 5 to 8 feet apart, plants 2 to 3 feet apart.

DEPTH: Slightly below soil line on stock.

HARVEST TIME: In early summer.

If red raspberries are scarce and prohibitive in the markets, black and yellow varieties are nonexistent. The only way you can enjoy these treats is to grow them yourself.

HOW TO GROW BLACK AND YELLOW RASPBERRIES
Cultivation is exactly the same as for red raspberries (preceding entry).

VARIETIES: Fallgold (yellow); Black Treasure (black); Allen (black).

SOURCES: W. Atlee Burpee Co., Warminster, Pennsylvania 18974, or Clinton, Iowa 52732; George W. Park Seed Co., Greenwood, South Carolina 29647.

Fruit Trees

"Imagine, you can pick your own fresh peaches right in your own backyard," say the mail order catalogs. The thought is very tempting, but be forewarned. The cultivation of all fruit trees requires a reasonable amount of time and yearly care. In order to grow edible fruit, you must prune, fertilize, and lime your trees annually and, most important, during the growing season, you *must* spray your trees at regular intervals. If you do not, you will have diseased, buggy trees, inedible fruit—and an ugly mess. But if you do assume the responsibility of proper care, the rewards are great indeed. There really is nothing quite like the taste of a vine-ripened peach, warm from the sun, picked right off your own tree. Flavor, sweetness, and juiciness are far superior to the supermarket varieties which have been picked and shipped green, ripening in their crates or even at home on top of your refrigerator.

During the past ten years or so, a minor revolution in home orchard gardening has taken place. These days more and more people are discovering the joy of growing fruit on their own *dwarf* fruit trees. Practically anyone with a backyard or even an apartment terrace can grow them.

In fact dwarf fruit trees have so proved their worth that today commercial growers throughout the country are planting them in their orchards. The unique qualities of these trees are accomplished by grafting the fruit variety onto a dwarf root stalk, limiting the size of the tree.

One positive factor in their favor is that maintenance of dwarf fruit trees is far easier than that of standard or semidwarf varieties. No need to purchase expensive commercial spray equipment or to climb wobbly ladders at pruning and harvest time. These trees grow to a height of only 8 to 12 feet, as compared to the 40-foot height of standard-size trees when they reach maturity.

Another is that dwarf fruit trees generally bear fruit within a year or two of planting. You don't have to wait 5 to 10 years, the usual bearing time of standard varieties, to enjoy the fruits of your labor.

Another asset is that you will be able to plant a greater number of trees in a given space. Most backyards may accommodate one or two of the standard specimens. However, by planting dwarf trees you can grow twenty-five specimens in a space 50 feet by 50 feet. This allows you far greater latitude in variety and allows for cross-pollination as well.

The yield of dwarf trees remains in bounds. A standard tree may yield as many as twenty-five bushels of fruit, usually all at once. Quite a harvest, *if* you plan on going into the fruit business; however, dwarf trees yield only from one to two bushels per year per tree when fully grown. By planting specimens which ripen at different times during the season, you can stretch out your harvest from midsummer to late fall—a far more sensible way to enjoy these luscious edibles.

As further inducement in growing them, their spring blossoms are spectacular, adding great beauty to your landscape design; in autumn their foliage is brilliant and varied in color.

And finally, you can select the varieties you wish to grow. Years ago, nearly a hundred different varieties of apples were available in the markets. Today there are perhaps four or five. Many European varieties and early American varieties are also available for you to grow. For example, have you ever seen mirabelle plums available anywhere in the United States? You can grow these delicious yellow plums, so favored by the French for eating, cooking, and making liqueurs, as easily as the standard variety, if you know the source for the trees.

All right, you've decided to plant a mini-orchard. Once

again, keep in mind that you must care for trees or you will have created a monster.

I'd advise you to start on a small scale and add to your orchard as you see fit. If you find that you enjoy growing your own fruit, you will undoubtedly add to your collection as the years pass. I have found that there is little more labor involved with twenty-five as with five or ten.

Order your trees in late winter by mail from any number of nurseries or buy them in early spring locally. For rare and fine varieties (which is, after all, what we are concerned about in this book), write to Henry Leuthardt Nurseries, Montauk Highway, East Moriches, New York 11940, and ask them to send you their catalog. *Whatever you do, don't be tempted by bargain stock!* Once you have planted your fruit trees, they will bear fruit for almost a lifetime. Good stock is your best investment.

When you order your trees, be aware of cross-pollination. Many fruit trees require that two varieties of the fruit be planted in order to assure pollination by the bees. For instance, in most cases, you must plant two varieties of apple, apricot, pear, cherry, and plum. Peaches and nectarines are usually self-fruitful. That is, a single tree is sufficient for pollination. *Be absolutely certain that you inquire about this when you purchase your stock.*

Plant your apples, pears, plums, apricots, peaches, and nectarines in early spring, that is about the same time that you plant onions, peas, and lettuce in your garden in your area. If you have purchased your trees by mail order, they will probably arrive at your door bare root—that is, wrapped in damp wood shavings so that the roots will stay moist. Unwrap them immediately. If you notice that the medium is dry and that the roots have dried out, place the trees in a pail of water. If any roots are broken, prune them off. Leave them in the water for 24 hours, no longer. Should the weather be bad, or if you do not have time to plant them the following day, heel them into the earth. To do this, dig a wedge-shaped trench in a sheltered shady spot, place your stock against the slanting side of the trench, and cover the roots with soil. They should survive there until you are ready to plant.

There's an old adage: "If you are planting a five-dollar plant, dig a ten-dollar hole." And so it is with fruit trees. To plant, dig holes 2 feet deep by 2 feet wide, spaced a minimum of 10 feet apart. As you dig, set the topsoil aside, discarding the subsoil.

Now mix the topsoil with one bushel of compost. *Do not, repeat, do not add manure to the soil mixture. Manure, especially fresh manure, will burn the tender roots.* Place your tree in the hole with the graft union a few inches above the level of the ground. The graft union is the knobby part of the trunk where the fruit variety has been grafted to the dwarfed root stock. This will probably be the depth at which the tree had grown in the nursery.

Shovel a sufficient amount of the topsoil-compost mixture into the hole to make a mound on which the tree will sit at the correct depth. Set the tree on the mound and spread the roots around the side of the mound. Fill about two-thirds of the hole with the topsoil-compost mixture and firm the earth.

At the same time, set a stake in the ground next to the tree on the side of the direction of the prevailing wind to support it during its young years. Tie the tree to the stake with a rope which has been threaded through a piece of garden hose. Next, pour in a pail or two of water to settle the soil. After the water has drained, fill in the hole completely with more of the compost-topsoil mixture.

Build a ridge of soil about 1 yard in diameter around the tree. This will act as a catch basin and will facilitate irrigation during the dry, hot summer months.

Then wrap the tree trunk with hardware cloth, tree wrap, or aluminum foil. This will protect your young tree from sun scald, borers, and rodents. Leave this protective wrapping on the tree for several years, particularly during the winter. Rabbits thrive on the young bark of fruit trees and if given a chance can completely girdle the trunk, killing the tree.

Each year, in late winter or early spring, work into the soil around each tree 1/2 coffee can of 5-10-5 fertilizer or organic mixture. If your soil is acidic, which you can determine by testing the pH of your soil, add some lime.

The following sections deal with the particular procedures of pruning, spraying, and harvesting of the various varieties of fruit trees.

Apples

⚘

HOW TO PRUNE APPLE TREES

When your dormant apple trees have arrived by mail, or if you have purchased them in a nearby nursery, follow the instructions for first-year pruning. Very often no pruning will be necessary. Check instructions from the grower carefully or ask at the nursery where you purchase your trees.

In subsequent years, prune apple trees only to shape them, to cut out crossing branches, or to remove winter- or storm-damaged branches. Since apples bear on the same branches year in and year out, pruning is not a major consideration. Prune in early spring when the trees are dormant and coat the wounds with tree paint.

HOW TO SPRAY APPLE TREES

In early spring when the trees are dormant, spray with a dormant oil spray. The reason for this is that any scale insects and larvae, which thrive on apple trees, will be smothered by the thin coating of oil you apply, but wait until the temperature warms up to about 40 degrees before you proceed.

To protect the bees do not spray apples or any other fruit trees when they are in bloom. After the petals have dropped, begin your summer program of regularly spraying every 10 to 14 days. An all-purpose garden spray is what you should use. Continue spraying throughout the summer and into the fall until about a week before harvest.

HOW TO THIN APPLES

To prevent an apple tree from bearing biennially and to produce well-developed fruit, do not permit too many apples to ripen on the tree. After the tiny apples have developed, there will be a period of natural fruit drop. When that is over, thin apples out to from 4 to 5 inches apart.

CULTIVATION AND WATERING OF APPLE TREES

Keep the area around your apple trees free from weeds. If you plant your tree in a lawn area, allow a circle of some 2 feet around the tree to remain free from grass. Mulch your tree during the summer. Straw, grass clippings, hay, or sawdust can be used. Spread it around the tree in a circle about 2 to 3 feet across, some 2 to 3 inches deep. Be sure to remove the mulch at different times throughout the year to ascertain whether or not it has become a nesting place for mice.

Do not overwater! Too much water harms the root system and prevents the trees from coming into bearing. Except during very dry weather, when you should provide a good watering once a week at night, avoid watering. More fruit trees are killed by overwatering than die from too little water.

GARDENER'S TIP 1
If there is a heavy snowstorm during the winter, be sure to wrap the lower branches of your apple trees with aluminum foil to prevent rodents from girdling branches.

GARDENER'S TIP 2
Almost all apples require another variety for cross-pollination. Consult your mail order house or nursery for recommended cross-pollination varieties.

SOURCE: Henry Leuthardt Nurseries, Inc., Montauk Highway, East Moriches, Long Island, New York 11940.

VARIETIES: DWARF APPLE

Summer Ripening—July 30–August 30

Chenango Strawberry—Yellowish white, striped with red; mild flavor, good for cooking, dessert. August.

Early McIntosh—A cross between regular McIntosh and Yellow Transparent; very similar to McIntosh. September.

Melba—Red, crisp, tender, juicy, good to very good. Mid-August–September.

Red Astrachian—Crisp, tender, early for cooking, later for dessert. July–September.

Yellow Transparent—Pale yellow; good but not high flavor, best for cooking. July–August.

Early Fall Ripening—September 1 to 30.

Baldwin—Yellow with red, crisp, tender, juicy, and very good. Keeps well.

Cortland—Few weeks after McIntosh in ripening; white crisp flesh, good for dessert and cooking.

Gravenstein—Orange yellow with red stripes. Crisp and very good to best. Keeps late September to early November.

McIntosh—Good deep red, dessert and cooking. Keeps October until December or beyond, if conditions are favorable.

Richard Delicious—Red, one of the best. Good color and flavor.

Yellow Delicious—Yellow, crisp, very juicy, and best as an eating apple.

Late Fall Ripening—October 1 to November 10.

Gallia Beauty—Red, very good for eating and cooking. Fruit large and crisp. Keeps October to January.

Jonathan—Brilliant red skin, firm but crisp. Juicy, good for cooking and dessert.

Macoun—Dark red and high quality. Similar to McIntosh but ripens considerably later than McIntosh.

Northern Spy—Red, tender, crisp, juicy. Very good to best for cooking or dessert. Keeps November to February.

Rhode Island Greening—Green, then yellow; good for dessert or cooking. Keeps October until March.

Winesap—Red, crisp, firm, juicy. Good to very good. One of the best keepers, from December to May.

RARE AND CHOICE DWARF APPLE:

Berne Rose—A Swiss apple similar to Baldwin but bears heavily every year. Keeps until April.

Black Gilliflower (Sheepnose)—Color, flavor, and aroma mark it as an unusual and attractive fruit. The tree is vigorous, healthy, and fruitful. Red deepening almost to black. Rich, mild sweet flavor; dessert, cooking, and keeping. October.

Calville Blanc—Yellow, high vitamin C content. Good eating. Keeps September to January.

Canada Reinette—Skin yellow with irregular patches of russet, firm, crisp, juicy, with distinct aroma. Keeps November to April.

Cox Orange—Beautiful to look at and delicious in taste, this is one of the choicest of apples. Orange-red deepening to bright red. Flesh yellow, firm, tender, and very juicy. Good to best eating. Keeps October to January.

Fameuse (Snow)—Red, very tender, and juicy. Flesh of snowy whiteness. Very good eating. Keeps October to January.

Gold Parmain—Yellow, red stripes. Crisp, a superior eating apple. September.

Golden Russet—Hardy, vigorous variety. Suffers little from pests. Keeps December to April. Yellow, crisp, very good for dessert and cooking.

Grimes Golden—Beautiful rich golden color. Firm but crisp and tender, pleasantly aciduous flavor, pleasant aroma. Very good to best. November to January.

Lady—Beautiful miniature fruits of highest quality. Suitable for dessert and decorative purposes. Deep red blush with yellow. Keeps December until May.

Ribston Pippin—Most exotic apple worth growing in America. The apples are not attractive, but have a fine rich flavor and pleasant aroma. Yellow, very crisp, good for cooking and dessert. Late September through December.

Roxbury Russet—Notable keeper. Remarkable for the amount of sugar contained. Fruit large, flesh yellow, firm. Good to very good. Keeps until May.

Spitzenberg—Flavor rich, spicy, and aromatic. Color deep yellow covered with bright red. Best for eating. September through January.

Tolman Sweet—Hardy, healthy, productive variety. Fruit attractive yellow color with a blush of red. Good quality. Best of the sweet apples. October.

COOKING TIP 1

You will undoubtedly have more than enough apples for eating, baking, and storing. I always peel a reasonable supply, slice them paper thin, and put them out on a screen in the sun to dry. Or you can dry them in a very slow oven. When they are bone dry, store them in airtight containers. During the winter, you can add them to hot cereals or soak them in a little boiling water and make applesauce out of them. You can also use them in stuffings for duck, chicken, turkey, or goose.

Beyond that, use the surplus to make your own apple butter. The store-bought variety is a far cry from homemade. True apple butter is made with apple cider and apples, not water. My favorite recipe for this classic American concoction appears in *The American Heritage Cookbook*.

Apricots

HOW TO PRUNE APRICOT TREES

Check instructions when your trees arrive or inquire from the nursery about pruning at planting time. Apricots probably require the least pruning of all fruit trees. Prune to shape, removing damaged limbs or crisscross branches. Be especially aware of crotches forming in the upper reaches of your trees. Remove the weakest of the branches and prune the others back by one-third. The reason for this is that apricot trees tend to be very brittle and may split during heavy winds. Prune in early spring when trees are dormant and coat wounds with tree paint or Elmer's glue.

Of late, another school of thought has surfaced regarding the pruning of apricot trees. There are those who feel that this tree, like peach and nectarine trees, should be severely pruned each year. That is, all new growth should be cut back by one-third in late winter. I have had great success with my apricot tree in terms of yield by following the traditional pruning process; however, if you find after three or four years that your trees are not bearing prolifically, you might wish to try the new approach.

HOW TO SPRAY APRICOTS

Use dormant oil spray in early spring to smother scale and larvae. Pick a day when the temperature is above 40 degrees. Spray again around mid-May with a fungicide such as Ferbam to avoid fungus diseases. Then spray every 10 to 14 days with all-purpose orchard spray during the season. Do not spray for about a week before harvest time.

HOW TO THIN APRICOTS
After fruit drop, thin to 3 inches apart.

CULTIVATION AND WATERING OF APRICOT TREES
As with all other fruit trees, keep the area beneath the tree weed-free, water only in drought, and mulch 2 to 3 inches.

GARDENER'S TIP 1
Apricot trees are especially brittle, so when your trees are young, provide support with a sturdy stake.

GARDENER'S TIP 2
Be sure to cover lower branches of trees with aluminum foil during winter storms to keep hungry rabbits from nibbling.

GARDENER'S TIP 3
Apricots are self-pollinating, so one tree is all you will need.

GARDENER'S TIP 4
Spring blossoms carry a heavy heady scent quite similar to jasmine. If you prune, be sure to bring the clippings inside to force for fragrant flowers.

VARIETIES: Goldcot, Hungarian Rose, Improved Moorpark, Stark Earli-Orange, Wilson Delicious.

SOURCE: Henry Leuthardt Nurseries, Inc., Montauk Highway, East Moriches, New York 11940; Stark Brothers, Louisiana, Missouri 63353.

COOKING TIP 1
The French prepare luscious apricot desserts using dessert rice cooked with boiled milk, sugar, butter, vanilla, and orange or lemon rind. Consult the *Escoffier Cook Book* for several delicious apricot dessert recipes.

Cherries

HOW TO PRUNE CHERRY TREES

Of all the fruit trees, cherries are, perhaps, the most risky to transplant. Check very carefully with the grower or nursery where you buy your stock about pruning instructions and follow them to the letter. If a nurseryman should tell you, "It doesn't matter whether or not you prune them," or if he shrugs his shoulders nonchalantly, run in the other direction—the man simply does not know his business.

Beyond that, after the tree is established and in early spring while it is still dormant, prune out lateral or side branches. You do this to prevent a crowded head and to develop desirable spacing of wide, single, lateral branches. Ideally your cherry tree should have four to five branches or laterals on the head of the tree. Coat tree wounds with tree paint. Also prune out all dead wood, branches that crisscross, and suckers.

HOW TO SPRAY CHERRY TREES

Use a dormant oil spray in early spring and all-purpose orchard spray every 10 to 14 days until about 1 week before harvest except when in bloom.

HOW TO THIN CHERRY TREES

Do not thin cherries when they form, unless the crop is definitely too thick.

CULTIVATION AND WATERING OF CHERRY TREES
Maintain a weed-free area beneath the tree, water during drought, and mulch 2 to 3 inches deep.

GARDENER'S TIP 1
Birds love cherries. In order to have any crop left for yourself, you may have to net the entire tree with plastic netting.

SOURCE: Henry Leuthardt Nurseries, Inc., Montauk Highway, East Moriches, New York 11940.

VARIETIES: Most cherry trees which you will find suitable for your garden are semidwarf, growing to from 9 to 12 feet.

Bing—Excellent dark red, nearly black cherry of the highest quality. This cherry is the one you find in the markets.

Black Tartarian—A medium-early, large, purplish black, tender juicy cherry. The tree is vigorous, a good bearer, and considered the best pollinator for other cherry trees.

Montmorency Sour Cherry—This cherry is light to dark red, tender, and slightly tart. Excellent for pies and pastries.

North Star—It grows only 6 feet tall and is self-pollinating. New.

Royal Anne—Large light-yellow cherries with bright red cheeks. These are juicy and sweet.

Schmidt's Biggereau—A dark red cherry that grows in clusters. The tree is hardy and very productive. This is the earliest of the large, hard-fleshed variety.

Windsor—This tree bears large fruit of an almost black color. It is late bearing. The tree is vigorous and a good pollinator.

COOKING TIP 1
Brandied cherries are a special treat. To make them, sterilize three 1-quart jars. Wash the cherries and wipe dry. You can either remove the stems or leave them on the fruit. In a medium-size saucepan, stir together 2 cups granulated sugar and 1/2 cup water. When the sugar is completely dissolved turn off the heat. Cool and stir in 1 quart brandy. Fill the jars with the cherries and cover with the brandy syrup. Then cut out three 4-inch circles of parchment paper. Crinkle them up and insert one into each bot-

tle. This will serve to keep the fruit below the surface of the syrup. Screw on the lids and store in a cool, dry spot for several weeks. Serve with duck, ice cream, or plain with whipped cream or crème fraîche.

COOKING TIP 2
Cold cherry soup is very refreshing at high noon in midsummer. An excellent recipe can be found in Craig Claiborne's *The New York Times Cookbook.*

Nectarines and Peaches

*

Instructions for the cultivation of nectarines and peaches are exactly the same.

HOW TO PRUNE NECTARINE AND PEACH TREES
There is a considerable amount more expertise involved in pruning peach and nectarine trees than in other stone fruits. The reason is that these trees bear fruit only on the previous year's growth, so your tree must be rejuvenated annually. Once you've been through the pruning process several times, you will not find it complicated at all.

When your trees arrive, check for pruning instructions on planting. In subsequent years prune your trees in late winter or early spring while still dormant. Here's what to look for:

1. Suckers. These are the branches that grow perpendicularly out of established branches, generally straight up into the air. Prune them all off.
2. Dead branches. These look dead and probably are. Cut them off.
3. For proper ripening, a peach or nectarine tree should resemble an upside-down umbrella, with plenty of breath-

ing space for air and sunshine in the middle. Cut out
center growing branches.

4. All fruit-bearing wood, that is the previous year's growth,
   should be cut back by from a fourth to one-third. If your
   tree is especially vigorous, you can even cut back by a
   half.
5. Bottom growth. Cut off all suckers that are growing at the
   base of the tree.
6. Beyond that, every four years or so, major limbs should
   be cut out so that new ones can replace them. You would
   do well at this point to consult a nursery or professional
   fruit grower for advice.

Keep in mind that it is near impossible to overprune a peach or
nectarine tree. Also, remember that if you don't prune reasonably
drastically, your tree will run out of steam in a relatively short
time and will have to be replaced. Be sure to coat all wounds with
tree paint.

HOW TO SPRAY NECTARINE AND PEACH TREES
Use dormant oil spray in early spring while trees are still dormant.
Use Ferbam or other fungicide around mid-May or when you set
out your tomato plants. After petals have dropped, spray every
10 to 14 days with all-purpose orchard spray.

HOW TO THIN NECTARINE AND PEACH TREES
Your trees will probably produce more fruit than your apple or
pear trees. After fruit drop, the natural thinning of the tree, thin
the set fruit to about every 4 inches.

CULTIVATION AND WATERING OF NECTARINE AND
PEACH TREES
As with all other fruit trees, keep surrounding areas free of
weeds, water only during serious drought, and mulch to a depth
of 2 or 3 inches.

GARDENER'S TIP 1
Protect your trees from rabbits during winter snowstorms. Wrap
aluminum foil around lower branches.

GARDENER'S TIP 2
Peaches and nectarines are self-pollinating. You do not need two
varieties to produce fruit; however, undoubtedly you will want
more than one of these.

GARDENER'S TIP 3
For sheer beauty, the deep pink blossoms of the nectarine are
breathtaking.

SOURCE: Henry Leuthardt Nurseries, Inc., Montauk Highway,
East Moriches, New York 11940.

VARIETIES: PEACHES
Belle of Georgia—The flesh of this peach is white. It is semi-
cling and of excellent flavor. The tree is not recommended for
colder areas, as it is somewhat fragile.
Elberta—A yellow-fleshed free-stone peach, this is the best
producer of high-quality fruit.
Golden Jubilee—Yellow, free-stone, large, juicy, very hardy.
Hale Haven—Yellow free-stone, good quality, high red
color. This tree is vigorous and productive.
Red Haven—Very early, yellow free-stone; medium to large
fine-flavored fruit. Very hardy. Bears 1 week before Golden Jubilee.
Red Skin—Cross between Hale and Elberta, ripening before
Elberta. The fruit is yellow-fleshed, firm, and very juicy.

NECTARINES
Hunter—The fruits are large and of very good quality, free
to semifree-stone, juicy, sweet, and tender.
Sure Crop—Large fruit with a bright red color, free-stone,
and of good quality.

COOKING TIP 1
The first time I visited Budapest and Warsaw, I discovered cold
fruit soups. Hungarians and Poles have a passion for them. Then,
while visiting North Carolina, I stopped in at a restaurant in New
Berne and lo and behold, a cold peach soup was served. It was
delicious. To make cold peach soup, simply take about 2 pounds
of very fresh, ripe peaches. Skin and slice them and purée them

in a blender. Add about 1 quart of half-and-half, 2 teaspoons of almond extract or almond liqueur, and sugar to taste. Chill to frigid and serve in chilled bowls. In Middle and Eastern Europe, they top these soups with a dollop of sour cream. If that is to your taste, just add the sour cream when you serve the soup. You can do the same thing with nectarines.

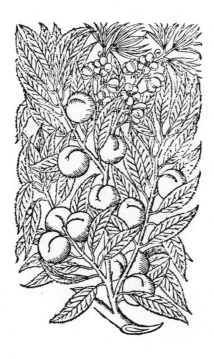

Pears

✑

As with apple trees, when your pears arrive by mail, or if you have purchased them in a nursery, follow instructions for first-year pruning. Very probably, no pruning will be necessary. Check with instructions from grower or ask at the nursery where you have purchased your stock.

Dwarf pears are slow-growing and require very little pruning. Prune only to shape the tree: remove damaged branches or those which crisscross each other. Pears, like apples, are borne on the same branches year in and year out, so pruning is not a major yearly task. Prune in early spring when trees are dormant and coat all wounds with tree paint.

HOW TO SPRAY PEAR TREES

When the trees are dormant in the early spring, spray with dormant oil spray. Choose a day when the temperature has warmed up to about 40 degrees. Like apples, pears are victims of scale. The dormant oil spray smothers these creatures.

When the petals have dropped, begin your yearly spray program. Spray trees every 10 to 14 days and continue to do so throughout the season until about 1 week before harvest.

HOW TO THIN PEAR TREES

Perhaps 3 to 5 years after you have planted your pear tree, it will begin to produce in abundance. After the natural fruit drop, thin pears to from 4 to 5 inches apart.

CULTIVATION AND WATERING OF PEAR TREES

As with apple trees, maintaining a weed-free area beneath your pear tree is important. Allow a circle of from 2 to 3 feet around the tree to remain free of grass and weeds. Mulch during the summer with straw, grass clippings, hay, or sawdust. The mulch should be 2 to 3 inches deep. Check at different times throughout the year to be sure mice have not made nests in it.

Do not overwater! As with most fruits, too much water can kill your pear trees. Do not water except in dry, hot spells and then only once a week.

GARDENER'S TIP 1

During heavy snows, wrap the lower branches of your pear trees with aluminum foil to about 2 feet above the level of the snow; otherwise, rabbits will nibble away, girdling the branches, perhaps killing your tree.

GARDENER'S TIP 2

As with apples, almost all pears require another variety for cross-pollination. Consult your nursery for recommended varieties.

GARDENER'S TIP 3

Fire blight is deadly to pear trees. If you have a problem with this disease in your locale, order only varieties of pear which are resistant to this disease. Check with your local state Agricultural Cooperative Extension to find out if your area is seriously affected by fire blight.

SOURCE: Henry Leuthardt Nurseries, Inc., Montauk Highway, East Moriches, New York 11940.

VARIETIES:

Bartlett—Large, handsome fruit with thin skin. Yellow when fully mature, ripening in September.

Beurre Bosc—Near-perfect fruits, tender buttery, very juicy, yellow with rust color. Ripens October to November.

Clapp's Favorite—This pear is similar to Bartlett, but ripens 1 week to 10 days before Bartlett with a slightly larger fruit.

Keiffer—A cooking pear that matures in late October and early November. It keeps well and is resistant to fire blight.

Moon Glow—This variety is resistant to fire blight. The fruit is soft, juicy with a mild flavor. Ripens in September.

Seckel—A small reddish brown pear, slightly spicy, juicy, ripening in October. Used mostly for canning and spiced pears.

Sheldon—An October-ripening pear with melting flesh. Good for dessert, keeps well. Russet color.

RARE AND CHOICE PEARS

Belle Lucrative—Small fruit, but the flesh and flavor are nearly perfect. The color is greenish yellow with small russet dots. Ripens in October.

Beurre Clairgeau—Large fruit, smooth rich and yellow at maturity. Fruit is granular, first firm and then tender and melting.

Conference—Fruit is long and arched, yellowish green, spotted with red. The flesh is fine, juicy, and sweet. Ripens in October.

Dr. Jules Guyot—Very large fruit with lemon yellow skin with a pink tinge. The flesh is tender, sweet, and juicy. Ripens in August.

Jargonelle—A first-quality strong-growing pear. Medium-size fruit ripens in August.

Louise Bonne D'Avranche—A strong upright-growing variety, red and yellow in color. The fruit is long, the juice of first quality. Ripens in October and is very productive.

Marguerite Marilate—Vigorous and productive grower with large fruit of excellent quality. Ripens in September.

Winter Nellis—A standard winter pear in the United States. The flesh is tender, melting, and juicy. Keeps well and ripens from late November to January.

COOKING TIP 1

I like fresh ripe pears served with Gourmandaise cheese, the walnut-flavored variety. William's Pear Brandy, with or without the pear in the bottle, is dry as a bone and accompanies the fruit and cheese nicely.

Plums

*

HOW TO PRUNE PLUM TREES

Check instructions from the nursery about pruning plum trees when your stock arrives by mail or when you purchase it at a nursery. Usually no pruning will be necessary.

Plums, like apples, pears, and apricots, require little pruning when young. Prune only to shape the tree, to remove winter or storm-damaged branches, or to cut out crossing branches which will rub against each other during windy periods. If a slingshot crotch forms at the top of the tree, remove the weaker branch and cut the other by a third. This will eliminate any danger of the tree splitting during wind storms. Prune in early spring when tree is dormant and cover wounds with tree paint.

HOW TO SPRAY PLUM TREES

Spray with dormant oil spray when tree is dormant and when temperatures climb to 40 degrees. Unlike pears and apples, plums should also be sprayed with a fungicide around the time you set out tomato plants. During the rest of the season, spray with all-purpose orchard spray, every 10 to 14 days. Stop spraying about 1 week before harvest.

HOW TO THIN PLUM TREES

Undoubtedly your plum trees will produce more fruit than is practical for the tree to support. After the natural fruit drop, thin fruit to every 4 or 5 inches.

CULTIVATION AND WATERING OF PLUM TREES

As with all other fruit trees, keep your surrounding area free of weeds, water only during serious drought, and mulch to a depth of 2 or 3 inches.

GARDENER'S TIP 1

In the winter, if there is a heavy snowfall, wrap all of the lower branches of your plum trees with aluminum foil to prevent rodent damage. Two feet above the snow level is a good height.

GARDENER'S TIP 2

Check for cross-pollination. Some varieties require another variety for cross-pollination; some do not.

GARDENER'S TIP 3

Plum blossoms carry a heavy, intoxicating fragrance. When you prune in spring, bring twigs indoors to force bloom.

SOURCES: Henry Leuthardt Nurseries, Inc., Montauk Highway, East Moriches, New York 11940; Stark Brothers, Louisiana, Missouri 63353.

VARIETIES: Blufre, Burbank Elephant Heart, Burbank Grand Prize, Burbank Red Ace, Stark Blue Ribbon, Starking Delicious, plus the following:

EUROPEAN PLUMS

German Prune—This is the oldest plum under cultivation. The color is purple, and it is free-stone. The ripening period is quite long.

Italian Prune—The fruit is finely flavored, very tart; flesh is yellow, juicy, and very good to eat. Free-stone.

Reine Claude (Green Gage)—Very juicy, rich in flavor, with tender melting flesh. The color is dull greenish yellow with green streaks. Ideal dessert plum.

Shropshire Damson—A medium-size plum of dark purple color which grows in clusters. Especially good for preserving. The tree is a good grower and very productive. Cling-stone.

Stanley Prune—This is the newest and most profitable commercial and home orchard variety. It is a very heavy bearer of excellent fruit.

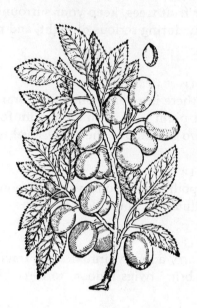

JAPANESE PLUMS

Abundance—This has an attractive dark red skin. It is of medium size, ripens early. The flesh is yellow, very juicy, and stone-clinging.

Burbank—These are medium-large, deep yellow marbled with red. They are sweet with yellow flesh and very prolific. Cling-stone.

Santa Rosa—Large round fruit of purplish red color, with yellow flesh. It is an early plum and is cling-stone.

SPECIALTY PLUMS

Imperial Epineuse—This plum has a reddish purple color. The flavor is exceptional, one probably not surpassed by any of our domestic grown varieties.

Mirabelle—In Europe, especially in France, this plum is much grown and highly esteemed. It is rarely seen in this country.

Fruits are used in tarts, compotes, and for canning. The small round yellow fruits are attractive in appearance and sweet and pleasant in flavor. There is no domestic plum like it. Ripens the end of August.

COOKING TIP 1
Plums are a favorite fruit in Europe and are used in a great many concoctions. Simply use a basic recipe for a Dutch apple cake, substituting fresh plum halves for apple slices.

COOKING TIP 2
Plum butter is perhaps my favorite way of using this fruit. It's easy to make. Simply cut up plums, skin and all, and combine 1 cup sugar for each cup of plums. Put the mixture in a large pot, stir well, bring to a boil, then simmer over very low heat until very thick. Be sure to watch the pot like a hawk to avoid burning. The simmering process will take about 2 hours. Pack in sterilized jars and seal.

Figs

HARDINESS: Perennial tree, tender. Needs protection during winter in areas where winter temperatures fall below 20 degrees.

WHEN TO PLANT: In spring after all danger of frost.

SPACING: 6 feet.

DEPTH: Soil line of stock.

HARVEST TIME: Second year when figs are ripe.

During the winter, in Mediterranean ethnic neighborhoods, you've probably seen large bushes wrapped in burlap or plastic to protect them from the frigid temperatures. They are probably fig trees, for these resourceful gardeners who hail from the sunny Mediterranean have found ways to grow these fruit as far north as Boston. With a little care and winter protection figs are easily grown in your own garden. As you undoubtedly are aware, they are rarely available in the markets.

HOW TO GROW FIG TREES
Since the plants are seldom available from a local nursery, the best source is a mail order nursery. Plant your fig tree in a container that can be moved into the house during the winter. If you

plant in the ground, try to locate your tree in a spot that is sheltered, sunny, with southern exposure.

Dig a large hole, some 2 feet wide by 18 inches deep. Place the topsoil to the side and discard the subsoil. Mix the topsoil with plenty of compost, rotted manure, some sand, and 2 cups of lime. Avoid using peat moss, as figs do not like acid soil.

If the tree is shipped dry root, prune away any injured roots, as well as about one-third of the top growth. Soak the plant in a bucket of water out of the sun for several hours.

Set the tree in the ground about 1 inch lower than it was in the nursery. Fill in half the hole with the soil mixture and pour a pail of water in to settle the soil. When the water has drained, fill the remaining half of the hole with the soil and tamp it down gently with your hands. Water again. Fill in later with additional soil and tamp down with your feet.

Should you decide on potting the tree, select a container 6 to 8 inches across, place gravel or flower pot shards in the bottom for drainage, and follow the same procedure as above. Next year repot in a 10- to 12-inch container.

In a few weeks, new shoots will appear. Water your tree regularly during the summer. Keep the area around the tree free of weeds and mulch with grass clippings.

In July, work a cup of 5-10-5 fertilizer or organic mixture into the ground around the tree. Nitrogen will cause excessive leaf growth and sparse fruiting. Next spring, and each thereafter, top-dress with compost and rotted manure and 1 cup of lime. In late August or early September, you will probably be able to pick a few figs. Next year, of course, you will have a bonanza.

Fig trees are relatively disease-free. However, a spring spraying of dormant oil spray to smother scale and other pests is sometimes recommended. If leaf curl appears, spray with Ferbam or general orchard spray about every 2 weeks.

In the fall, before freezing, winterize the tree. Judiciously prune it to manageable size. Then tie the branches together, but be careful not to break them in the process. Place piles of leaves at the base, wrap the tree with insulation bats, and tie them together.

Cover the entire wrapped tree with plastic (an old shower curtain works well) or burlap and tie that in place. Be sure that your wrapped tree is waterproof, as ice within will wreak havoc.

Next spring after danger of frost is over, unwrap the tree and prune any broken branches. You will not be pruning away bearing stock, as figs bear on the current year's growth.

If you have potted your fig tree, simply move it indoors before frost. When growth begins in the spring, move to a sunny window, water regularly, and mist. After all danger of frost, place it outdoors buried in the soil to pot level. Or if you have a broad sunny terrace, the fig tree can be used as a decorative accent.

GARDENER'S TIP 1
Reliable mail order nurseries will not ship fig trees after the end of May or beginning of June, so if you decide to plant one, order early.

VARIETIES: There are several, but specify your area in your order and leave the selection up to the nursery. They know what will grow best in your location.

SOURCES: Van Bourgondien Brothers, 245 Farmingdale Road, P.O. Box A, Route 109, Babylon, New York 11702; W. Atlee Burpee Seed Company, Warminster, Pennsylvania 18991.

COOKING TIP 1
We've all enjoyed the delicious combination of prosciutto and melon, but have you ever thought of serving prosciutto with fresh figs? Simply quarter the figs, wrap each with a slice of prosciutto, and serve chilled. It's an interesting variation on the classic.

A FINAL POSTSCRIPT
ON FRUIT TREES

Just a little bit of advice about spraying. If you follow instructions for each individual variety of tree and try to set up a spraying schedule, you will drive yourself crazy. One variety should be sprayed every 10 days, another every 7, another every 14, some 2 days after petal drop, some 2 weeks after fruit set, etc. I have had excellent results by spraying all of my fruit trees regardless of variety on a regular 10- to 14-day schedule. If the weather forecast calls for rain, wait until after the rainfall to spray. And if you have just sprayed and have a heavy downpour, you would do well to respray your entire orchard.

"Don't sit under the apple tree . . ." or the pear tree or any other fruit tree when fruit is near ripe. A falling apple can cause an injury to your head.

Nut Trees

Growing nut trees is a project not to be taken lightly, for many years are often required to bring a small tree to bearing size. Further, most varieties of nut trees require a great deal of space. However, if you have the patience to wait for your crop and the acreage to allow for their space needs, you will be rewarded with a bonanza of delicious nuts. And you can grow many native American varieties of nuts that are never available in the markets. For example, have you ever tasted a butternut? Butternut trees are a native American species that used to be abundant but are rarely grown these days.

HOW TO GROW NUT TREES

Instructions for growing most nut trees are similar. To assure success, be sure that the planting hole is both deep and wide enough to accommodate all roots. Do not cramp them. A good rule of thumb is to dig the hole two times the width and depth of the root ball. Since roots grow downward, place the topsoil, enriched with compost and peat moss, in the bottom of the hole. Enrich the subsoil as well, then cut back all injured roots to clean wood, but do not cut back the healthy roots. Never cut back roots to fit a small hole. Dig a larger hole.

When you plant, try to place the roots in as natural a position as possible. Fill in the hole with your enriched soil and tamp firmly on the soil after planting. Then fill the hole with water, let it sink in, and fill it again. Stake the new tree until the new roots have developed (two years is not an unreasonable length of time). Wrap the trunk with tree wrap available at garden centers to protect against sunscald and rodent damage.

You might also want to place a circle of chicken wire around the tree as further protection against hungry rabbits during winter. They find the bark of young trees irresistible; given a chance, they will girdle trees, eventually killing them.

The only other thing to remember about caring for and ultimately harvesting nut crops is squirrels. They have an insatiable appetite for these morsels. The best solution to this problem is to watch the crop like a hawk and, when it is ready, harvest immediately and beat the little devils to it.

Nut trees are usually pest- and disease-free. If problems arise, and they rarely do, you would be advised to call in professional tree experts.

Black Walnuts

Truly one of the most valuable and beautiful native trees, black walnuts grow rapidly to a majestic height of 70 to 100 feet or more. The nuts are about 2 inches thick, and the feathery foliage provides a not too heavy shade. The trees are virtually pest-free. Since their taproots grow to great depths, deep loamy soil is preferred. If your local water table is high, the trees may not thrive, as black walnuts require a deep, well-drained soil. Black walnuts do not survive in northern climates. Check locally for further information.

GARDENER'S TIP 1

Black walnuts possess the baffling quality of roots which can be toxic to some other trees and shrubs. Also be sure not to plant them near vegetable or flower gardens, foundation plantings, or even a fruit orchard. Evergreens are especially susceptible; however, lawn grass does not appear to be.

GARDENER'S TIP 2

Shelling black walnuts can be a chore. One solution is to lay the harvest out in the driveway and drive a car over the nuts once or twice. Then gather them up and remove the meats from the shells. Slamming car doors on the nuts is another recommended method.

Butternuts

Perhaps the richest and best-flavored of all the northern nuts, the butternut is not grown as much as it should be. The shells are quite tough, and the meat is not especially large, perhaps accounting for its scarcity. However, the delectable tidbits are worthy of planting space if you have substantial acreage. The foliage, providing light shade, is similar to that of the black walnut, although smaller. Growing 40 to 90 feet tall, it is hardy even in much of Canada.

Butternuts have long taproots, so a large, deep planting hole is essential. When selecting a site, plan on planting two specimens for cross-pollination, if space permits, although this is not usually necessary. Place the trees at least 35 feet apart and the same distance from other trees on the property. A sheltered spot is preferable, as a late spring frost can kill the blossoms. Soil should be fairly moist and not too acid. Butternut trees bear in eight to twelve years.

GARDENER'S TIP 1
As with black walnuts, shelling can be tedious. Use the same method as described in the preceding section on black walnuts.

Chinese Chestnuts

Since the native American chestnut trees have been destroyed by disease, the Chinese species has come to the fore. Chinese chestnuts will grow wherever peaches thrive. The trees require light, well-drained soil and room to spread their wide branching habit. To ensure good pollination, plant two or more and select from some of the newer hybrids offered.

The trees are applelike in shape and size and require no unusual care.

VARIETY: Chinese Chestnut.

SOURCE: Stark Brothers, Louisiana, Missouri 63353.

Hardy Hazelnut

Perhaps the most "sensible" of the nut trees to grow are the filberts or European hazels, for this plant is small, growing only to 10 or 12 feet. At waist level, the lanky trunks average only a few inches in diameter, with the branches light and shrubby in appearance. You can plant these in a shrub border without disturbing growing conditions for other shrubs. In early spring, hanging catkins, similar to those found on birch trees, grow from the branches. The trees are not fussy about soil. Average, well-drained soil enriched with compost and humus suffices. They will tolerate light shade. In the North, plant in a sheltered spot, since late spring frost can kill the blossoms. Remember to plant two or more trees for adequate cross-pollination.

GARDENER'S TIP 1
Hazelnuts tend to grow into bush form, so unless you want to create a hedge or windbreak, start pruning young saplings to tree form after their first year. This is simply a matter of pruning suckers at the base of the tree as they appear.

GARDENER'S TIP 2
Harvesting should start during the third year, with irregular harvesting after that.

Shagbark Hickory

This is a large sturdy shade tree which ultimately towers to between 80 and 100 feet. Though not as fast growing as black walnut, it is handsome full grown. Plant about 40 feet from other trees. Hickories have deep taproots and need a deep planting hole enriched with humus and well drained. Harvest will begin in about 3 years.

GARDENER'S TIP 1
The secret to cracking hickory nuts is to do so end to end, not lengthwise.

Carpathian Persian Walnut

A near-perfect shade tree, this strain of walnut originated in the Carpathian Mountains of Poland. Hardy to 40 degrees below zero, it thrives in a northern climate, is practically impervious to disease, grows in a symmetrical form, and has sturdy wind- and ice-resistant limbs. In addition, the tree does not produce gnarled roots at its base, saving possible knicks in the blades of a power mower. In the summer, the dark green tropical-looking leaves flutter in the summer breezes. In fall, of course, there is a bonanza of tasty walnuts.

Carpathian walnuts grow into rather large specimens. Be sure they have space, at least 40 feet apart. For proper pollination, two trees are a must. Since they have fairly long taproots, plant these walnuts deeply in a well-drained soil. Before planting work a substantial amount of compost, bonemeal, and humus into the soil and, if possible, plant the trees in a sheltered location. The trees should begin to bear in 4 to 7 years. By the time the tree is about 13 years old, it should yield three to four bushels of nuts per tree.

Hardy Pecan

The pecan tree thrives in the warm climate of America's South and Southwest. Some mail order houses offer "northern" varieties. However, while most of these are plant hardy, they rarely produce nuts in the most northerly states, for our seasons are too short and pecans need a long season to produce and properly mature.

VARIETIES: Missouri Hardy Pecan, Stark Surecrop Pecan, Starking Hardy Giant Pecan, Schley Paper Shell Pecan, Stuart Paper Shell Pecan.

SOURCE: Stark Brothers, Louisiana, Missouri 63353.

Almond

Do not try to grow almond trees unless you live in the South, unless you wish to do so experimentally. For those so inclined, some New York State nurserymen now offer some so-called hardy almonds.

SOURCES: Nurseries which purvey nut trees include: Stark Brothers Nurseries, Louisiana, Missouri 63353; W. Atlee Burpee Co., Warminster, Pennsylvania 97321, or Clinton, Iowa 18974; J. E. Miller Nurseries, Canandaigua, New York 14424; Van Bourgondien, Babylon, New York 11702.

Index

alfalfa sprouts, 102–103
alfalfa sprouts finger sandwiches, 103
almonds, 229
alpine strawberries, 171–173
American Heritage Cookbook, The, 193
Amstel carotes, 20–22
anise seed, 123–124
aphids, 65
apples, 189–193
  drying of, 193
  varieties of, 191–193
apricots, 194–196
arugula, 3–5
  serving of, 4–5
asparagus, 6–10
  blanched, 7–8
Asparagus à la flamande, 9
asparagus beans, 11–13
  pickled, 13
  stir-fried, 13
asparagus beetles, 9
asparagus rust, 9

basil (basilicone), 125–127
bean leaf beetles, 53, 92
bean rust, 52
beans:
  asparagus, 11–13
  French bush green, 51–53
  haricots verts, 51–53
  Romano, 91–92
  yard-long, 11–13
beets:
  Belgian, 14–16
  Middle European-style, 16
Belgian beets, 14–16
Belgian carrots, 20–22
Belgian carrots julienne, 22
Belgian Cookbook, The (Hazelton), 134
Belgian endive, 41
Bermuda onions, 75
berries, 159–182
Better Than Store-Bought (Colchie and Witty), 35
blackberries, 161–163
black walnuts, 221–222
  shelling of, 222

Blair, Sue, 35
blanched asparagus, 7–8
blossom-end rot, 24, 40, 79, 108
blueberries, 164–166
blueberry pie, 166
Bocuse, Paul, 136
bok choy, 17–19
  in cold bay scallop salad, 19
  in egg drop soup, 18–19
borers, 176
bottle onions, 74–75
brandied cherries, 198–199
Bruneau, Restaurant, Brussels, 9
butternuts, 223
  shelling of, 223

cabbage loopers, 65
cantaloupe, 70
cantaloupe sherbet, 72
caraway seeds, 128–129
  hors d'oeuvre spread, 129
  serving of, 129
Carpathian Persian walnuts, 227
carrot caterpillars, 22
carrots, Belgian, 20–22
catnip, 130–131
  serving of, 131
cayenne peppers, 23–25
  drying of, 25
celeriac, 26–27
  as garnish, 27
Chateau du Domaine de St. Martin, Vence, 53
cherries, 197–199
  brandied, 198–199
  as cold soup, 199
  varieties of, 198
cherry tomatoes, 112–114
chervil, 132–134
Chinese cabbage, 28–29
  as substitute for grape leaves, 29
Chinese chestnuts, 224

Chinese hot and sour soup, 67
Chinese Lion's Head soup, 29
chives, 135–137
chung choy, 110–111
Claiborne, Craig, 199
Classic Italian Cook Book, The (Hazan), 44, 101, 117
Colchie, Elizabeth, 35
Colorado potato beetles, 58
corn, 30–32
  honey and cream, 30–32
  serving of, 30
  silver queen, 30–32
corn earworms, 32
cornichons (gherkin pickles), 33–35
  serving of, 33, 35
corn salad, 68–69
crème fraîche, 173
cress, 36–37
  Danish, 36–37
cress finger sandwiches, 37
currants:
  black, 167
  red, 168–170
currant syrup, 170
cutworms, 24

daikon-carrot hot salad, 85
Day, Avanelle, 90, 176
day lilies, 66
dill, 138–139
  kosher pickles, 139
dow gauk, 11–13

eggplant, 38–40
  Japanese, 38–40
  serving of, 40
  white, 38–40
Egyptian onions, 76–77
elephant garlic, 45–47
endive (escarole), 41–42
escarole, 41–42

Escoffier Cook Book, 119, 196
essence of shallot, 95
Esterhazy, Count Peter, 181
European corn borers, 32

fenugreek sprouts, 102–103
Ferriere, Dominique, 53
figs, 212–214
    planting of, 212–214
    with prosciutto, 214
fingerling potatoes, 56–58
finocchio (fennel), 43–44
    serving of, 44
fish mousse in leeks, 61–62
flea beetles, 29, 114, 116
Florence fennel, 43–44
Four Seasons (restaurant), New York City, 101
fraises de bois, 171–173
French breakfast radishes, 86–87
French bush green beans, 51–53
fruit soups, cold:
    blackberry, 163
    cherry, 199
    peach, 202–203
fruit trees, 183–215
    cross-pollination of, 187
    dwarf varieties of, 185–186
    planting of, 187–188
fusarium wilt, 70

garlic, elephant, 45–47
gherkin pickles (cornichons), 33–35
ginger and scallion sauce, 50
ginger root, 48–50
globe onions, 75–76
gooseberries, 174–176
    serving of, 176
grated horseradish, 55
Gro-Lux, 116
Grillot, Luc, 53

haricots verts, 51–53
    serving of, 53
hatchet soup, 21
Hazan, Marcella, 44, 101, 117
hazelnuts, hardy, 225
Hazelton, Nika, 134
herbs, 121–157
hickory, shagbark, 226
hickory nuts, cracking of, 226
horseradish, 54–55
    grated, 55
    sauce, 55
hot and sour soup, Chinese, 67
Hungarian-style mushrooms, 80
Hungarian wax peppers, 78–80

Key to Chinese Cooking, The (Kuo), 29, 50, 98, 111
Kipfel Kartoffels (potatoes), 56–58
kirsch, in desserts, 72
kosher dill pickles, 139
Kuo, Irene, 29, 50, 98, 111

ladyfinger potatoes, 56–58
lamb's lettuce, 68–69
Larousse Gastronomique, 35, 42
leaf hoppers, 29
leaf miners, 15, 40
leaf spot, 15
leeks, 59–62
Le Pigeonneau, Aix-en-Provence, 22
lettuce, 63–65
    cos, 63
    head, 63
    leaf, 63
lily buds, 66–67
Lion's Head soup, Chinese, 29

mâche, 68–69
mâche summer salad, 69
melon Charantais, 70–72

Meridien Copacabana Hotel, Rio de Janeiro, 136
mesclum, 134
Mexican bean beetles, 53, 92
Mexican garlic soup, 47
Middle European-style beets, 16
mint, 140–142
    serving of, 142
    varieties of, 140
mixed salad sprouts, 102–103
mousse of scallops with beurre blanc sauce, 136–137
mung bean sprouts, 102–103
mushrooms, Hungarian-style, 80
muskmelon, 70

nectarines, 200–203
New York Times Cookbook, The (Claiborne), 199
nightshade, 57
Nouvelle Cuisine of Jean and Pierre Troisgros, The, 44, 65, 136
nut trees, 217–229
    planting of, 219–220

onion maggots, 61
onions, 73–77
    Bermuda, 75
    bottle, 74–75
    Egyptian, 76–77
    globe, 75–76
    walking, 76–77
oregano, 143–144
    use of, 144
Oriental daikon, 84–85

pak choi, 17–19
paprika peppers, 78–80
    drying of, 80
parsley, 145–146
    French curled, 145–146
    Italian, 145–146
    serving of, 146

parsleyworm, 146
peaches, 200–203
    cold soup, 202–203
    varieties of, 202
pears, 204–207
    serving of, 207
    varieties of, 205–207
peas, 81–83
    petits pois, 81–83
    snow, 96–98
    sugar snap, 104–106
pea weevils, 82–83, 97, 105
pecans, hardy, 228
peppers:
    cayenne, 23–25
    Hungarian wax, 78–80
    paprika, 78–80
    red, 78–80
    tabasco, 107–109
pesto, 127
petits pois, 81–83
    serving of, 83
pickled asparagus beans, 13
pickles, kosher dill, 139
Plaza-Athenée Hotel, Paris, 6
PLM Ile Rousse, Bandol, 53
plum butter, 211
plum cake, 211
plums, 208–211
    varieties of, 209–211
potage germiny, 118
potatoes:
    fingerling, 56–58
    Kipfel Kartoffels, 56–58
    ladyfinger, 56–58
potato salad, 58

radishes, 84–85
    French breakfast, 86–87
    Oriental daikon, 84–85
    serving of, 87
    winter, 84–85

raspberries:
  black, 182
  red, 177–181
  yellow, 182
raspberry crown borer, 180
raspberry vinegar (vinaigre de framboise), 180–181
raspberry vinegar sauce, 181
red peppers, 78–80
rhubarb, 88–90
rhubarb punch, 90
Ritz Hotel, Paris, 119
rocket, 3–5
Romano beans, 91–92
  serving of, 92
Roma tomatoes, 115–117
root maggots, 85, 87
roquette, 3–5
rosemary, 147–148
  serving of, 148

sage, 149–150
  serving of, 150
salads:
  hot daikon-carrot, 85
  mâche summer, 69
  potato, 58
  tomato-onion, 76
sauces:
  horseradish, 55
  raspberry vinegar, 181
scale, 176
schav, 118–119
seed maggots, 83, 98, 105
sesame seeds, 151–152
  serving of, 152
shagbark hickory, 226
shallots, 93–95
  essence of, 95
Sheraton Hotel, Paris, 69
siew choy, 28–29
snow peas, 96–98
sole with chives, 136

sorrel, 118–119
sorrel soup, 118
soups:
  blackberry, 163
  cherry, 199
  egg drop, 18–19
  hatchet, 21
  hot and sour, 67
  Lion's Head, 29
  Mexican garlic, 47
  peach, 202–203
  potage germiny, 118
  sorrel, 118
sourgrass, 118–119
spaghetti squash, 99–101
Spice Cookbook, The (Day and Stuckey), 90, 176
spices, 121–157
sprouts, 102–103
  alfalfa, 102–103
  fenugreek, 102–103
  mixed salad, 102–103
  mung bean, 102–103
squash bugs, 34, 72
squash vine borers, 34, 72
stir-frying:
  asparagus beans, 13
  daikon, 85
  mung bean sprouts, 103
  Tokyo turnips and snow peas, 111
strawberries, alpine, 171–173
striped cucumber beetles, 34, 72
Stuckey, Lillie, 90, 176
sugar snap peas, 104–106
  serving of, 106

tabasco peppers, 107–109
tabasco sauce, 108–109
tarragon, 153–154
tarragon vinegar, 154
thrips, 61

thyme, 155–157
  serving of, 157
  varieties of, 155–156
Tokyo turnips, 110–111
tomatoes:
  cherry, 112–114
  Roma, 115–117
tomato hornworms, 114, 116
tomato-onion salad, 76
Troisgros, Jean and Pierre, 27, 44

vinaigre de framboise (raspberry
  vinegar), 180–181

walking onions, 76–77
walnuts:
  black, 221–222
  Carpathian Persian, 227
white pine blister rust, 167,
  175
winter radish, 84–85
wireworms, 22
witloof, 41
Witty, Helen, 35

ya choy, 28–29
yard-long beans, 11–13

About the Author

THEODORE JAMES JR. is a regular contributor to the *New York Times* gardening section and to such magazines as *Better Homes and Gardens, Town and Country, Cosmopolitan* and *Smithsonian.* He makes his home on the north fork of Long Island, where he has an eighteenth-century house and, as he puts it, "an acre of the best soil this side of Kansas." With such fertile land to work with and his own deep love of gardening, it was natural that he would create a garden any plant-lover—and food-lover—would envy. To gather much of the information for this book, James traveled to farming regions all over the world.

A Note about the Type

The text of this book was set in a computer version of Palatino, one of the type faces designed by Hermann Zapf, the renowned German calligrapher and typographer. Zapf's first designs for the face were made in 1948 and complete fonts were issued between 1950 and 1952. The face was named after Giovanbattista Palatino, an Italian writing master of the Renaissance, which is fitting since the italic is strongly calligraphic in style. The entire font of Palatino is noted for its beauty, clarity and elegance.

The book was composed by ComCom, Allentown, Pennsylvania, printed and bound by The Book Press, Inc., Brattleboro, Vermont.

The book was designed by Earl Tidwell.